FRENCH
for
COMMUNICATION

Workbook, Level I

by

Gary A. Milgrom
Françoise Santalis

Copyright © 1993
CURRICULUM PRESS, INC.
Guilderland, New York

ISBN 0-941519-15-5

Printed in the United State of America

TABLE OF CONTENTS

CORRECTIVE, UNIT I   NAME_____

I. Topic: *Qui es-tu?*

A. FIRST STUDY Aim I, pages 3-5, Aim II, pages 6-8, Aim IVB, pages 13-14, and Aim VA and VB, pages 14-18.

B. The following are answers which John gave to Ann's questions. Write the questions which Ann asked.

1. **Anne:** Bonjour! _____?
    Jean: Ça va bien merci.

2. **Anne:** _____?
    Jean: Je m'appelle Jean.

3. **Anne:** _____?
    Jean: Je suis des Etats-Unis.

4. **Anne:** _____?
    Jean: J'ai quinze ans.

5. **Anne:** _____
    _____?
    Jean: Mon numéro de téléfone
    est 592-7384.

C. Answer the following questions in French. Give your own answers.

1. Quel âge as-tu? _____
2. Comment vas-tu? _____
3. D'où es-tu? _____
4. Comment t'appelles-tu? _____
5. Quel est ton numéro de téléphone? _____

D. Your teacher or peer partner will ask you five questions. After the second repetition of each question, answer with a complete sentence in French.

1. _____
2. _____
3. _____
4. _____
5. _____

CORRECTIVE, UNIT I

NAME_____

II. Topic: *Les numéros: Quel âge as-tu?*

A. FIRST STUDY Aim VA, pages 14-16 and Aim VIA, pages 18-19. Be able to state all the numbers from 0 - 20.

B. Then write the number which **follows** each number. (For example, *deux* follows *un.)*

un, _deux_ ; trois, _____; cinq, _____; sept, _____; neuf, _____;

onze, _____; treize, _____; quinze, _____;

dix-sept, _____; dix-neuf, _____

C. Your teacher or peer partner will tell you the ages of seven people. After the second repetition of each number, write the age of each person in Arabic numbers.

1._____ 2._____ 3._____ 4._____ 5._____ 6._____ 7._____

III. Topic: *Les numéros de téléphone*

A. FIRST STUDY Aim VB, pages 16-18 and then review **Topic II** of this Corrective.

B. Write the following telephone numbers in French words.

1. 590-3264 _____

2. 843-7961 _____

C. Your teacher or peer partner will tell you the telephone numbers of three people. After the second repetition, write each telephone number in Arabic numbers.

1. _____ 2. _____ 3. _____

IV. Topic: *Les numéros*

A. FIRST STUDY Aim VA and VIA, numbers 0-20 and models of addition and subtraction on pages 15 and 19.

B. Then write the following math problems in French words followed by each answer.

1. 5 + 14 = _____
2. 20 - 12 = _____
3. 13 - 6 = _____
4. 11 + 4 = _____
5. 17 - 7 = _____

CORRECTIVE, UNIT I NAME_____

V. Topic: *Une conversation entre ... et ...*

A. FIRST STUDY all the Aims of Unit I which you have not studied already including Aim III, pages 8-9.

B. Write four ways you have learned to say good-bye.

1. _____ 3. _____

2. _____ 4. _____

C. Fill in the blanks of this conversation between John and Ann.

1. **Jean:** Bonjour! _____?
   Anne: Ça va bien. Et toi?

2. **Jean:** _____.
   _____?
   Anne: Je m'appelle Anne. Et toi?

3. **Jean:** _____.
   _____?
   Anne: J'ai quinze ans. Et toi?

4. **Jean:** _____.
   _____?
   Anne: Je suis des Etats-Unis. Et toi?

5. **Jean:** _____.
   Quel est ton numéro de téléphone?
   Anne: _____
   _____.

6. **Anne:** Il est tard *(It's getting late.)*
   Au revoir, Jean.
   Jean: _____, Anne.

CORRECTIVE, UNIT I

NAME_____

VI. Topic: *Où est-ce qu'on parle français?*

A. Study the location of each of the French-speaking countries of the Western Hemisphere on the map of Aim IVA, page 10. Write the name of each country next to the letter it represents.

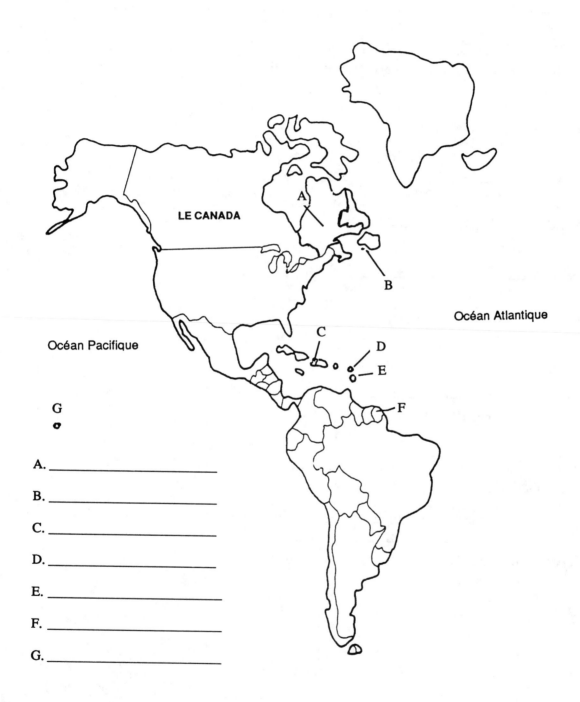

A._____

B._____

C._____

D._____

E._____

F._____

G._____

ENRICHMENT, UNIT I NAME_____

I. *Le prénom*

Do you know how to say your name in French? Not all English names have a French equivalent. Look for your name on the following list. If it is not on the list, choose a French first name that you like or that begins with the same letter as your first name.

A. Complete only **one** of the following statements:

My name in French is _____.

The name I would like to be called in French is _____.

Les prénoms de garçons:

Albert *Albert*	Stéphane *Steven*	Manuel *Manuel*
Alexandre *Alexander*	Eugène *Eugene*	Marc *Mark*
Alfred *Alfred*	Frédérique *Frederick*	Michel *Michael*
Adré *Andrew*	Philippe *Philip*	Nicola *Nicolas*
Arnold *Arnold*	François *Francis*	Paul *Paul*
Benjamin *Benjamin*	George *George*	Patric *Patrick*
Bernard *Bernard*	Guillaume *William*	Pierre *Peter*
Charles *Charles*	Hector *Hector*	Rafaël *Raphael*
Christophe *Christopher*	Herbert *Herbert*	Richard *Richard*
Jean *John*	Joachin *Joaquin*	Xavier *Xavier*
Edouard *Edward*	Joseph *Joseph*	
Henri *Henri*	Louis *Louis*	

Les prénoms de filles

Adèle *Adele*	Hélène *Helen*	Joséphine *Josephine*
Aïda *Aida*	Henriette *Henrietta*	Julie *Julia*
Alice *Alice*	Ester *Esther*	Laure *Laura*
Anne *Ann*	Eve *Eva*	Eléonor *Eleanor*
Barbara *Barbara*	Florence *Florence*	Louise *Louise*
Blanche *Blanche*	Françoise *Frances*	Madeleine *Madeline*
Charlotte *Charlotte*	Irène *Irene*	Nicole *Nicole*
Caroline *Caroline*	Isabelle *Isabel*	
Catherine *Catherine*	Jeanne *Jean*	
Claire *Claire*		
Christine *Christine*		
Diane *Diana*		
Dorothée *Dorothy*		

ENRICHMENT, UNIT I   NAME_____

I. Le prénom (continued)

B. Puzle *(Wordsearch):*

Find 11 French first names of boys given on the list on the previous page. Circle the names you find and write them in the blanks.

```
O R M A R C U I H M O M
Z P H I L I P P E U V O
A L F R E D O R N E Y R
B O C A R P I E R R E Z
A B H D E F G H I E J K
J E A N M I C H E L L E
C H R I S T O P H E R A
O A L B E R T I N A B E
S U E U G E N E L F Q G
X Y S Z L P N M O D E C
```

1. _____
2. _____
3. _____
4. _____
5. _____
6. _____
7. _____
8. _____
9. _____
10. _____
11. _____

Find 12 French first names of girls given on the list on the previous page. Circle the names you find and write them in the blanks.

```
O B A L I C E O P J D M
R O B E R T A M A Z O U
A B N C L D E R A N L F
G H N E A G K A L I I R
E V E G P I R E N E C M
L W X Y Z M B A O R O A
D I A N E C H A S A L R
T U C H R I S T I N E I
A L E L O U I S E T T E
B A R B A R A V A I D A
```

1. _____
2. _____
3. _____
4. _____
5. _____
6. _____
7. _____
8. _____
9. _____
10. _____
11. _____
12. _____
13. _____

ENRICHMENT, UNIT I   NAME_____

I. Le prénom (continued)

C. Write the French first name of five of your male and female friends:

1._____   2. _____   3. _____   4. _____   5._____

D. Write the French first name of five members of your family or relatives:

1._____   2. _____   3. _____   4. _____   5. _____

II. Lettres mélangées (Word scramble):
Unscramble the following words and expressions of greeting, health and leave-taking.

1. R O U B N O J   _ _ _ _ _ _ _ _!
2. U T V S A T E N M M O C   _ _ _ _ _ _ _ _ _ _ _ _ _ _?
3. E D A L A M S I U S E J_ _ _ _ _ _ _ _ _ _ _ _ _.
4. N E I B A V A Ç   _ _ _ _ _ _ _ _ _ .
5. R G E R A L U   _ _ _ _ _ _ _ _.
6. F T A G I U É   _ _ _ _ _ _ _.
7. B E I N S É R T   _ _ _ _ _ _ _ _ _ _.
8. A T Ô T B E N I   _ _ _ _ _ _ _ _ _ _.
9. R I O V E R A U   _ _ _ _ _ _ _ _ _.
10. N I A M E D A   _ _ _ _ _ _ _ _ _.

III. Le numéro de téléfone de mon ami(e) ____ est ____.

Write the telephone numbers of five of your friends. Write five complete sentences stating the names of your friends and then the telephone numbers **in French words.** *Example:*

Le numéro de téléphone de mon ami Jean est sept-trois-zéro-quatre-huit-un-neuf.
Le numéro de téléphone de mon ami Hélène est _____.

1. _____
   _____

2. _____
   _____

3. _____
   _____

4. _____
   _____

5. _____
   _____

ENRICHMENT, UNIT I

NAME_____

IV: *Le jeu des carrés* (The game of Squares)

General rules for all square games to be played by two players are as follows. This game is similar to TIC-TAC-TOE. One player uses the circle "0" as his symbol, and the other player uses an "X". The first player selects any square, and first says and then writes the answer. If both players agree that the answer is correct, player #1 places his symbol in that box. Player #2 then has a turn. If an incorrect answer is given, it must be erased or crossed out, and the box remains open. The first player to get 3 symbols horizontally, vertically or diagonally is the winner. **Important:** Each player must state the **complete** math problem in French and then answer in French.

1

8+3=	16-4=	15+5=
16-2=	20-9=	7+6=
7+10=	18-13=	12-3=

2

17+2=	20-10=	16-12=
15+3=	19-5=	9+4=
14-5=	2+6=	11+8=

In the boxes below make up your own math problems and then play the game of Squares.

3

4

ENRICHMENT, UNIT I   NAME_____

V. *Mon ami(e) ... a ... ans*

Write the ages of five of your friends in French words. ***Examples:***

Mon ami Paul a douze ans.
Mon amie Jeanne a seize ans.

1. _____
2. _____
3. _____
4. _____
5. _____

VI. *On parle français dans de nombreux métiers / professions*

French is spoken in many jobs. List in English ten jobs in which being able to speak and understand French would be helpful.

1. _____   6. _____
2. _____   7. _____
3. _____   8. _____
4. _____   9. _____
5. _____   10. _____

ENRICHMENT, UNIT I   NAME_____

VII. *Un voyage* (a trip)

You have just won a trip to your choice of any of the French-speaking countries of the Western hemisphere!

A. Write the names of all the countries or provinces *and their capitals* (use an atlas or a classroom map) in the spaces provided below.

	pays	capitale
1.	_____	_____
2.	_____	_____
3.	_____	_____
4	_____	_____
5.	_____	_____
6.	_____	_____
7.	_____	_____

B. Write a brief essay about the country or region you have chosen to visit. Explain your reason for making this choice. Include geography, climate, culture, and places of interest.

_____
_____
_____
_____
_____
_____
_____
_____
_____
_____
_____
_____
_____
_____
_____

VIII: *Une conversation incomplète* (An incomplete conversation)

A conversation between two young people who are meeting for the first time has been recorded. However, the tape recorder did not work very well and parts of their conversation have been left out. Your task is to fill in the missing words or expressions to make the conversation complete.

1. **Charles:** Bonjour. _____ ça va?

2. **Pierre:** Ça va _____ bien. Et ____?

3. **Charles:** _____ aussi.

4. **Pierre:** Comment _____ tu?

5. **Charles:** _____ m'appelle Charles. _____ toi?

6. **Pierre:** _____ m'appelle _____.

7. **Charles:** _____ as-tu?

8. **Pierre:** _____ quatorze ans. _____ et-toi?

9. **Charles:** _____ de Bruxelles. Quel est _____ numéro ___ téléphone?

10. **Pierre:** Mon numéro de téléphone est 852-3049.

11. **Charles:** ___ bientôt, Pierre.

12. **Pierre:** _____, Charles.

IX: *La première rencontre* (The first meeting)

A. A new student has just arrived from Brussels, the capital of Belgium. Follow the cues in numbers 1 - 7 by giving or obtaining information. Partners take turns playing each role.

1. Greet him
2. Ask him how he is
3. Introduce yourself
4. Ask him his name
5. Ask him where he is from
6. Ask him how old he is
7. Ask him his telephone number

B. After both partners have taken turns playing the roles above in Part **A,** write numbers 1 - 7.

1. _____

2. _____

3. _____

4. _____

5. _____

6. _____

7. _____

SITUATIONS ORALES, UNIT I   NAME_____

I.

Function: Socializing
Roles: I am a new student in your class.
Purpose: You want to get to know me. You will begin.

1. **Toi:** _____

   L'élève: Ça va.

2. **Toi:** _____

   L'élève: Je m'appelle Anne Dupuis.

3. **Toi:** _____

   L'élève: J'ai quinze ans.

4. **Toi:** _____

   L'élève: Je suis de la Martinique.

5. **Toi:** _____

   L'élève: Au revoir. A demain.

II.

Function: Providing and Obtaining information
Roles: I am a student you meet in Quebec.
Purpose: I want to get to know you. I will begin.

1. **Un jeune homme ou une jeune fille:** Comment t'appelles-tu?

   Toi: _____

2. **Un jeune homme ou une jeune fille:** D'où es-tu?

   Toi: _____

3. **Un jeune homme ou une jeune fille:** Quel âge as-tu?

   Toi: _____

4. **Un jeune homme ou une jeune fille:** Quel est ton numéro de téléphone?

   Toi: _____

5. **Un jeune homme ou une jeune fille:** A bientôt.

   Toi: _____

Note: During this activity pairs of students will work together. To provide for sufficient "task" practice toward the goal of oral proficiency, each *situation* can be done two times with partners changing roles.

CORRECTIVE, UNIT II   NAME_____

V. *Qui es-tu?*

A. FIRST STUDY Aim IB, page 29, Aim II, pages 31-32, Aim III, pages 33-34, Aim IV, pages 35-37 and Aim V, pages 40-42, 46.

B. Then write the appropriate questions which were asked by Jean after reading the responses of Rose.

1. **Jean:** Bonjour! _____ ?
   Rose: Ça va bien, merci.

2. **Jean:** _____ ?
   Rose: Je m'appelle Rose.

3. **Jean:** _____ ?
   Rose: J'ai quinze ans.

4. **Jean:** _____ ?
   Rose: Mon anniversaire est le onze janvier.

5. **Jean:** _____ ?
   Rose: Je suis née en 1975.

6. **Jean:** _____ ?
   Rose: J'habite dans la ville de New York à Brooklyn.

7. **Jean:** _____ ?
   Rose: Mon numéro de téléphone est 765-2948.

8. **Jean:** _____ ?
   Rose: Je suis sympathique, petite, athlétique et mince.

9. **Jean:** _____ ?
   Rose: J'aime nager, jouer au tennis, faire la cuisine et écouter la radio.

C. Answer the following questions with a complete sentence in French.

1. Comment ça va? _____

2. Comment t'appelles-tu? _____

3. Quel âge as-tu? _____

4. Quand est ton anniversaire? _____

5. En quelle année est-tu né (née)? _____

6. Quel est ton numéro de téléphone? _____

7. Où habites-tu? _____

8. Comment es-tu? (5) _____

9. Qu'est-ce que tu aimes faire? (5) _____

_____

D. Your teacher or peer partner will ask you five questions of personal identification. Answer each with a complete sentence.

1. _____

2. _____

3. _____

4. _____

5. _____

ENRICHMENT, UNIT II   NAME_____

I. *Les jours de fêtes en France*

A. Write the dates in French of the following French holidays.

1. le jour de l'an *(New Year's Day)*

    January 1 _____

2. la fête nationale
    (Bastille day)

    July 14 _____

3. la fête du travail *(Labor day)*

    May 1 _____

4. Pâques
    (Easter)

    (Current year) _____

5. Noël   *(Christmas)*
    December 25 _____

6. La Toussaint
    (All Saints day)
    November 1 _____

7. La Pentecôte
    (Pentecost)

    (Current year) _____

8. La fête des Mères *(Mother's day)*

    (3rd Sunday in May) _____

9. La fêtes des Pères
    (Father's day)

    (1st Sunday in June) _____

10. Jeudi de l'ascension *(Ascension day)*

    (11 days after Easter) _____

11. L'armistice   *(Armistice day)*

    November 11 _____

12. L'assomption *(Assumption day)*

    August 15 _____

II. *Les jours de fêtes aux Etats-Unis*

Write the names (in English) of 6 holidays in the United States **not** celebrated in France, or that are celebrated on a different date. Write the dates in French.

1. Martin Luther King's Birthday   _____
2. _____   _____
3. _____   _____
4. _____   _____
5. _____   _____
6. _____   _____

ENRICHMENT, UNIT II   NAME_____

III. L'anniversaire de mon ami(e) est le _____ _____

Write the birthdays of five of your friends. **Examples:**

L'anniversaire de mon ami Jean est le premier décembre.
L'anniversaire de mon amie Marie est le treize août.

1. _____
2. _____
3. _____
4. _____
5. _____

IV. Addition et soustraction en français (Adding and subtracting in French)

Write in French words the following math problems of addition and subtraction and the answer to each problem.

1. 36 + 27 = _____
2. 91 - 12 = _____
3. 14 + 42 = _____
4. 88 - 75 = _____
5. 55 + 15 = _____

V. Puzle

Find the infinitive (the dictionary form) of the verb which
we use after the expressions *J'aime...* and *Je n'aime pas...*
First write each infinitive in French in the blank and then
circle each one that you find.

to dance _____
to sing _____
to travel _____
to buy _____
to swim _____
to walk _____
to work _____
to make _____
to like _____
to play (the guitar)

_____

to listen to (the radio)

_____

to speak (on the telephone)

_____

```
A  D  A  N  S  E  R  Y  P  R  S  U  T  N  H  O  P  Z
C  O  U  A  M  C  W  Z  A  L  M  E  R  S  T  S  V  O
O  Q  A  G  J  O  U  E  R  O  A  M  A  R  C  H  E  R
L  M  S  E  K  U  N  V  L  E  P  V  B  D  H  C  F  L
S  T  O  R  I  T  A  Z  E  Q  M  E  A  T  A  U  X  R
U  Z  U  L  J  E  L  O  R  S  V  G  I  W  N  V  S  O
Z  A  I  M  E  R  U  P  K  W  O  H  L  Q  T  R  M  Y
G  I  K  S  B  A  E  I  J  E  Y  K  L  S  E  L  U  Z
J  H  A  O  F  I  J  E  L  P  A  M  E  P  R  O  A  E
O  L  E  N  M  U  K  P  O  R  G  N  R  F  I  L  S  W
N  J  A  S  L  A  C  H  E  T  E  R  O  G  E  A  T  B
Y  B  L  U  O  R  M  S  U  E  R  N  Z  J  R  N  U  A
F  A  I  R  E  X  L  F  C  N  O  P  R  Z  N  E  O  L
```

NAME_____

VI. *Le candidat*

You are a candidate for political office. There are so many French-speaking voters that you find it advisable to campaign in French as well as in English. Describe your personal, physical and psychological characteristics for the voters. State a minimum of 15 adjectives in French which describe you. **Note:** five of them must be words that do **not** appear in this unit. Look them up in a dictionary.

1. Je suis _____
2. _____
3. _____
4. _____
5. _____

6. _____
7. _____
8. _____
9. _____
10. _____

11. _____
12. _____
13. _____
14. _____
15. _____

VII. *Le jeu des "carrés"* (The game of Squares)

General rules for all square games to be played by two players are as follows. This game is similar to TIC-TAC-TOE. One player uses the circle "0" as his symbol, and the other player uses the "X". The first player selects any square, and first says and then writes in French whether s/he likes or dislikes to do the activity in the box chosen. If both players agree that the statement is correct, player # 1 places his/her symbol in that box. Player #2 then has a turn. If an incorrect statement is given, it must be erased or crossed out., and the box remains open. The first player to get three symbols horizontally, vertically or diagonally is the winner. **Important:** Each player must give the statement in a complete sentence in French.

1

2

ENRICHMENT, UNIT II   NAME_____

VIII. *Ce que je connais au sujet d'Anne* (What I know about Ann)

The following information was told to you about Ann. Rewrite this information **as if Ann were telling you about herself.**

1. Elle s'appelle Anne.   Je m'appelle Anne._____
2. Elle a quinze ans. _____
3. Son anniversaire est le premier août. _____
   _____
4. Elle est née le premier août 1975. _____
   _____
5. Elle est du Québec. _____
6. Elle habitr à Miami en Floride. _____
7. Elle aime nager et danser. _____
8. Elle est petite, mince et bonne. _____

IX. *Je suis ou je ne suis pas...* (I am or I am not...)

A. Before each characteristic listed indicate whether you possess that characteristic (*Je suis...*) or not (*Je ne suis pas...*). When two forms of the characteristic are listed, be sure to answer using the appropriate one according to your gender (male or female).

1. _____ expressif.
   _____ expressive.
2. _____ actif.
   _____ active.
3. _____ créatif.
   _____ créative.

4. _____ spontané.
   _____ spontanée.
5. _____ agressif.
   _____ agressive.
6. _____ organisé.
   _____ organisée.

7. _____ ambitieux.
   _____ ambitieuse.
8. _____ aventureux.
   _____ aventureuse.
9. _____ indépendent.
   _____ indépendente.

10. _____ arrogant.
    _____ arrogante.
11. _____ patient.
    _____ patiente.
12. _____ persistent.
    _____ persistente.

13. _____ honnête.
14. _____ romantique.
15. _____ idéaliste.

16. _____ responsable.
17. _____ dynamique.
18. _____ pessimiste.

19. _____ optimiste.
20. _____ timide.

You know the meaning of many of these words because of their similarity to English. These words are called "cognates". Cognates are words which, due to their common origin, look alike, have the same meaning and often sound alike in two languages.

ENRICHMENT, UNIT II   NAME _____

B. Studying a second language which has cognates with English can help us increase our vocabulary in both languages. Write the English meaning of ten of the words in Part A. Write both the French word and its English meaning.

1. _____

2. _____

3. _____

4. _____

5. _____

6. _____

7. _____

8. _____

9. _____

10. _____

C. Look up in the dictionary the meaning of any five words from Part A whose meaning you do not know or are not sure of. Write both the French word and its English meaning.

1. _____

2. _____

3. _____

4. _____

5. _____

SITUATIONS ORALES, UNIT II   NAME _____

A. Function: Information
Role: I am an French-speaking exchange student in your school.
Purpose: You are interviewing me for the school paper. You will begin.

1. **Toi:** Comment t'appelles-tu?
   L'élève: _____.

2. **Toi:** Où habites-tu?
   L'élève: _____.

3. **Toi:** Quel âge as-tu?
   L'élève: _____.

4. **Toi:** Comment ça va?
   L'élève: _____.

5. **Toi:** Qu'est-ce que tu aimes faire?
   L'élève: _____.

B. Function: Socializing
Role: I am your friend's parent whom you are meeting for the first time.
Purpose: Tell me about yourself. You will begin by introducing yourself.

Note: During this activity pairs of students will work together. To provide for sufficient "task" practice toward the goal of oral proficiency, each *situation orale* can be done two times with partners changing roles.

26

Notes

CORRECTIVE, UNIT III   NAME _____

I. Topic: *Quel temps fait-il?*

A. FIRST STUDY the weather expressions, Aim IB, pages 53-57 and the temperatures, Aim IA, pages 51-52. Then write the weather condition represented by each of the following pictures in the blanks provided.

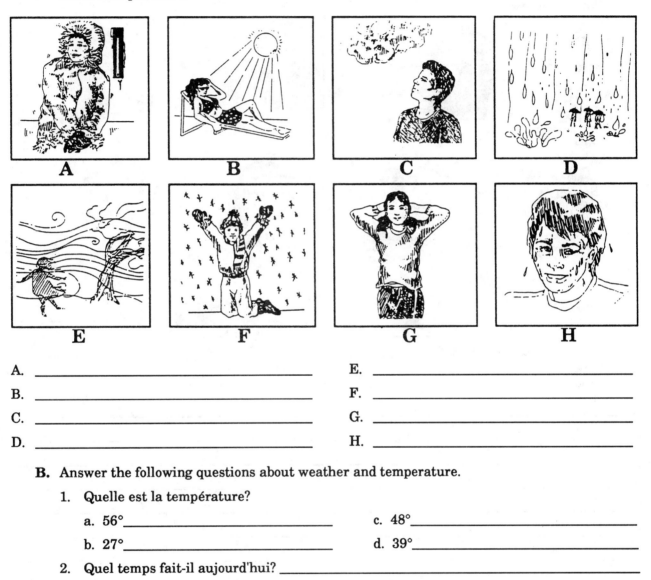

A. _____   E. _____

B. _____   F. _____

C. _____   G. _____

D. _____   H. _____

B. Answer the following questions about weather and temperature.

1. Quelle est la température?

   a. 56°_____   c. 48°_____

   b. 27°_____   d. 39°_____

2. Quel temps fait-il aujourd'hui? _____

II. Topic: *Les salutations*

Study greetings, Aim IV, pages 65-67 ("Note", page 65). How would you greet an adult or stranger at these times?

1. at 9:30 p.m.? _____   3. at 7:15 a.m.? _____

2. at 4:00 p.m.? _____   4. at 6:20 p.m.? _____

CORRECTIVE, UNIT III   NAME_____

III. Topic: *Qu'est-ce que ... aime faire?*

A. FIRST STUDY the 10 activities which a person might like or not like to do,
Aim V, pages 68-71.
B. Next write whether you like or don't like to do each of the activities represented by each
picture below.

1   2   3   4

5   6   7   8

9   10

1. _____

2. _____

3. _____

4. _____

5. _____

6. _____

7. _____

8. _____

9. _____

10. _____

IV. Topic: *Qui êtes vous?*

A. FIRST STUDY the basic questions of personal identification which you would ask of an adult, Aim VI, pages 73-75.

B. Read the following responses of Mrs. Grassin to Helen's questions. Now write the questions which Helen asked.

1. **Hélène:** _____

   Mme Grassin: Je m'appelle Françoise Grassin.

2. **Hélène:** _____

   Mme Grassin: Je suis du Québec.

3. **Hélène:** _____

   Mme Grassin: J'habite á Los Angeles en Californie.

4. **Hélène:** _____

   Mme Grassin: J'ai trente-trois ans.

5. **Hélène:** _____

   Mme Grassin: Mon anniversaire est l'onze janvier.

6. **Hélène:** _____

   Mme Grassin: Je suis née en 1957.

7. **Hélène:** _____

   Mme Grassin: Mon numéro de télephone est 784-5679.

8. **Hélène:** _____

   Mme Grassin: Pendent mon temps libre j'aime lire, aller au cinéma, danser, écrire des lettrese et jouer au tennis.

C. Answer all the questions (1 - 8) that you have just written as if you had been asked them.

1. _____
2. _____
3. _____
4. _____
5. _____
6. _____
7. _____
8. _____

V. Topic: *Un dialogue entre ... et ....*

A. Study the greetings and read the dialogues of Aim IV, *Exercice orale* page 65. Next read the *Note culturelle* page 67 and study the *Vocabulaire* on the same page.

B. Next fill in each blank with an appropriate expression from the choices given:

> *Bonjour. / Je suis très fatiguée. / Et vous? / A bientôt.*

> *Bonsoir./ Je suis très fatigué. / Et toi?*

(It is 3:00 p.m.)

Jacqueline: Comment allez-vous M. Durand?

M. Durand: _____ . _____?

Jacqueline: Je suis un peu malade.

M. Durand: _____, Jacqueline.

Jacqueline: Au revoir, Monsieur Durand.

VI. *Les saisons*

A. Study the seasons of the year, Aim II, pages 58-61 including *Exercice orale 2,* page 59. Then answer the following:

1. Quel temps fait-il en été? _____

2. Quel temps fait-il en automne? _____

3. Quel temps fait-il en hiver? _____

4. Quel temps fait-il au printemps? _____

5. Quelle est ta saison favorite? Pourquoi? _____

_____

CORRECTIVE, UNIT III   NAME_____

VII. Topic: *Où parle-ton français?*

A. FIRST STUDY the name and location of each French-speaking country,
Aim II, pages 62-64.
B. Then write the name of each country next to the number to which it corresponds on the
following map.

On parle français en:

1. _____   5. _____

2. _____   6. _____

3. _____   7. _____

4. _____   8. _____

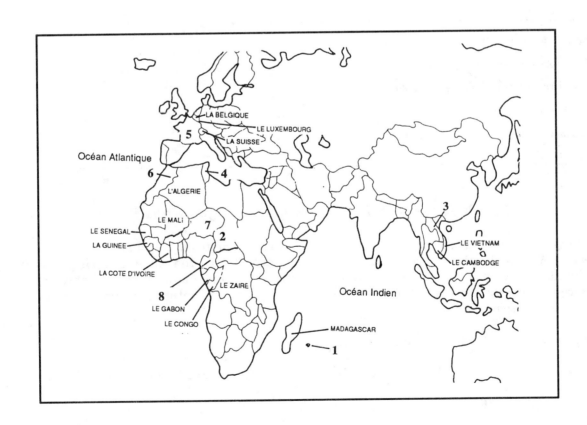

ENRICHMENT, UNIT III   NAME_____

I. Lettres mélangées (Word scramble)

Unscramble the following letters to form weather expressions:

1. LI   TAIF   DUACH   _ _   _ _ _ _ _
2. LI   IAFT   DROIF   _ _ _ _ _ _ _ _ _
3. LI   LEUTP   _ _   _ _ _ _ _ _
4. TAS   DEVONIOP   _ _ _   _ _ _ _ _ _ _ _ _
5. IRAT   NOVET   _ _ _ _   _ _ _ _ _
6. AF   VOTITAC   MOTEP _ _   _ _ _ _ _ _ _ _   _ _ _ _ _
7. EC   LSEO   _ _   _ _ _ _
8. Af   SCORFE   _ _   _ _ _ _ _ _
9. ANCIVE   _ _ _ _ _ _ _

II. Ma saison favorite

1. Quelle est ta saison favorite?

   _____.

2. Quels sont les mois de ta saison favorite?

   Le mois de _____ sont_____ , _____ et _____.

3. Quel temps fait-il dans ta saison favorite?

   En _____ il fait_____ et il fait _____.

4. Qu'est-ce que tu aimes faire dans ta saison favorite?

   _____

   _____

III. Quel temps fait-il à Lyon, France pendant l'année

Many American tourists visit France during the year and quite often include Lyon on their itinerary. Will you be able to understand the weather report? Since the temperature is given in Centigrade, follow the simple formula given to find out the approximate equivalent Fahrenheit temperatures during the year. To find Farenheit, when given the Centigrade temperature, double the Centigrade temperature and add 30.

Example: For the month of January: 2 x 13 = 26 + 30 = 56

	Jan	Feb	Mar	Apr	May	June	July	Aug	Sept	Oct	Nov	Dec
C	8	12	16	18	21	24	27	29	26	22	19	13
F	46	_	_	_	_	_	_	_	_	_	_	_

ENRICHMENT, UNIT III   NAME_____

IV. Squares

This game is similar to TIC-TAC-TOE. One player uses the circle "0" as his/her symbol, and the other uses the "X". Each player first **states** (in French) and then **writes** (in French) whether s/he likes or dislikes the activity in the box chosen. Players take turns.

#1

#2

ENRICHMENT, UNIT III   NAME_____

V. *Jeu de découverte* (Unit III, page 72)

Choose five activities you **like to do** from the list below and use each in a complete sentence.

1. _____
2. _____
3. _____
4. _____
5. _____

Oui or *Non* answers to be recorded before each activity according to your partner's answers:

_____ aller à la plage	_____ jouer au baseball	_____ jouer au football
_____ voyager	_____ aller au cinéma	_____ chanter
_____ lire le journal	_____ jouer de la guitare	_____ aller aux parties
_____ ècouter la radio	_____ regarder la télévision	_____ parler au téléphone
_____ nager	_____ manger	_____ acheter de la nourriture
_____ faire des exercices	_____ travailler	_____ danser
_____ marcher	_____ écrire des lettres	_____ donner des cadeaux
_____ dormir	_____ sortir avec un ami (ou une amie)	_____ courir

ENRICHMENT, UNIT III   NAME_____

VI.

You have just won a trip to five French-speaking countries of your choice.

A. Identify each French-speaking country indicated by a number on the map below. Write the name of each region in its appropriate column labeled *pays*.

B. Your airplane will land in the capital of each country. Write the name of each capital in the appropriate column labeled *capitale*. You may consult an atlas, globe or a map in the encyclopedia.

pays

1. _____
2. _____
3. _____
4. _____
5. _____

capitale

1. _____
2. _____
3. _____
4. _____
5. _____

ENRICHMENT, UNIT III   NAME _____

VII. *Les pays que je veux visiter* (The countries I want to visit)

Choose two of the five French-speaking countries which you may want to visit in the future. Write five items of information which you have learned about each region after consulting an encyclopedia or other reference work.

Pays # 1 _____

1. _____
   _____
2. _____
   _____
3. _____
   _____
4. _____
   _____
5. _____
   _____

Pays # 2 _____

1. _____
   _____
2. _____
   _____
3. _____
   _____
4. _____
   _____
5. _____
   _____

VIII. The art of France

France is well known for its art. Choosing Paris or another French city, do a research report on the places (museums, galleries, etc.) where one might find works of art displayed. Include in your report brief biographies of the artists as well as descriptions of their specific works.

_____

_____

_____

_____

_____

_____

_____

_____

_____

_____

_____

_____

_____

_____

_____

_____

_____

_____

_____

_____

_____

_____

_____

_____

ENRICHMENT, UNIT III   **NAME** _____

IX. *Une interview* (An interview)

In the following interview Mr. Smith was applying for a job with the United States Government, requiring a knowledge of French. You are asked to listen to a tape of that interview. However, the interviewer's questions were not recorded clearly on the tape. Write a transcript of the interview filling in the missing questions.

1. **Mme Chibault:** _____
    M. Smith: Je vais bien, merci.

2. **Mme Chibault:** _____
    M. Smith: Je m'appelle Robert Smith.

3. **Mme Chibault:** _____
    M. Smith: Je suis etes Etats-Unis, de la Florida.

4. **Mme Chibault:** _____
    M. Smith: Jái vingt-huit ans.

5. **Mme Chibault:** _____
    M. Smith: J'habite dans la ville de Cleveland, Ohio.

6. **Mme Chibault:** _____
    M. Smith: Mon numéro de telephone est 867-9403.

7. **Mme Chibault:** _____
    M. Smith: Pendant mon temps libre jáime lire des romans, ecrire des poèms, faire des exercices
    et voyager dans les pays où lón parle francais.

8. **Mme Chibault:** _____
    M. Smith: J'aime voyager l'été.

9. **Mme Chibault:** _____
    M. Smith: Mon pays favori est le Québec.

10. **Mme Chibault:** _____
    M. Smith: Parceque les Québecois sont sympathiques. Québec est une ville trés jolie
    et j'aime la neige.

11. **Mme Chibault:** _____
    M. Smith: Oui, j'aime beaucoup lire les journeaux. Je lis en anglais et en françois.

12. **Mme Chibault:** M. Smith, vous parlez très bien français. La place est à vous.
    M. Smith: Merci beaucoup, Mme Chibault.

ENRICHMENT, UNIT III   NAME _____

X. *Trouver la personne...* (Find the person ...)

You are going to interview several "strangers" in the class to find out information of personal identification. The goal of this activity is to see who can get the most questions answered on this interview sheet. You will have about fifteen minutes. **Speak to only one person at a time.** Ask each person a specific question such as *"Vous habitez près de l'école?"* The person addressed must answer in a complete sentence: *"J'habite près de l'école,"* or *"Je n'habite pas près de l'école."* When you get a "yes" answer write the person's name in the space provided and move on to another person. Use a person's name only once and find one person for each question on the sheet.

Trouver la personne...

1.   ...qui habite près de l école. _____

2.   ...qui aime faire la cuisine. _____

3.   ...qui n'est pas des Etats Unis. _____

4.   ...qui aime lire le journal. _____

5.   ...qui est née au mois d'août. _____

6.   ...qui n'aime pas parler au téléphone. _____

7.   ..qui est intelligente, jeune et sympathique. _____

8.   ..qui n'aime pas l'hiver. _____

9.   ...qui est très fatigué(e). _____

10. ...qui aime jouer la guitare ou du piano. _____

Vocabulaire:
près de   *near*

SITUATIONS ORALES, UNIT III   NAME_____

A. Function: Expressing feelings
   Role: I am your friend.
   Purpose: We are discussing which time of year is our favorite. I will begin the conversation.

1. **L'ami(e):** Quelle est ta saison favorite?

   Toi: _____.

2. **L'ami(e):** Pourquoi est-ce que tu aimes...?

   Toi: _____.

3. **L'ami(e):** Quel temps fait-il en ...?

   Toi: _____.

4. **L'ami(e):** Quést-ce que tu aimes faire en ...?

   Toi: _____.

5. **L'ami(e):** Quelle saison est-ce que tu n'aimes pas? Pourquoi?

   Toi: _____.

B. Function: Socializing
   Role: I am your friend's parent whom you are meeting for the first time.
   Purpose: You want to ask me a few questions to get to know me. You will begin.

1. **Toi:** _____ ?

   Le père/La mère: Je vais très bien, merci.

2. **Toi:** _____ ?

   Le père/La mère: Je m'appelle Jean Perrin / Je m'appelle Anne Dupon.

3. **Toi:** _____ ?

   Le père/La mère: Je suis ete Belgique.

4. **Toi:** _____ ?

   Le père/La mère: J'habite à Bruxelle dans la rue de la Paix.

5. **Toi:** _____ ?

   Le père/La mère: Pendant mon temps libre j'aime aller à plage, nager, lire le journal

   et écouter de la musique.

C. Function: Providing and Obtaining Information
   Roles: I am a French businessperson who is returning home after a business trip to the
   United States.
   Purpose: You are taking your vacation in France. We meet on the airplane and you begin
   the conversation by introducing yourself to me.

CORRECTIVE, UNIT IV   NAME_____

I. Topic: *Les objets de la classe*

A. FIRST STUDY the French names of some basic objects and materials commonly found in the classroom, Aim I, pages 81-84. Then write the name of each object in French next to its corresponding letter indicated in the picture on page 83. In each answer write the appropriate indefinite article, *"un"* or *"une"*, before the object given.

Est...   Est...   Est...

B. _____   H. _____   O. _____

C. _____   I. _____   Q. _____

E. _____   K. _____   R. _____

F. _____   L. _____

G. _____   M. _____

B. Study the questions and sample answers on page 82, **Conversation 1** and **2**. Then answer the following questions according to the cues given (*Oui ou Non*).

1. Est-ce que tu as un livre? Oui, _____

2. Est-ce que tu as une craie? Non, _____

3. Est-ce que tu me prêtes le crayon? Oui, _____

4. Est-ce que tu me prêtes la gomme? Non, _____

5. Est-ce que tu me prêtes le livre? Je suis navré. _____

II: Topic: *Qu'est-ce qu'on fait dans la classe?*

FIRST STUDY what each person usually does in the classroom, Aim IIA, pages 84-87 and the *Vocabulaire* on pages 87-88. Then answer each question with a complete sentence. Refer to pages 88-89 for the pictures to be used for this exercise.

A. Que fait Robert?
   Il passe un examen.

B. Que fait l'élève?
   Elle parle français.

C. Que fait le garçon?
   _____

D. Que fait le professeur?
   _____

E. Que fait Michel?
   _____

F. Que fait la fille?
   _____

G. Que fait Jean?
   _____

H. Que fait l'élève?
   _____

I. Que fait la fille?
   _____

J. Que fait le professeur?
   _____

K. Que fait Marie?
   _____

L. Que fait le garçon?
   _____

III. Topic: *Les jours de la semaine*

A. FIRST STUDY the days of the week in French, Aim III, pages 96 and 99. Be able to recite them. Then fill in the blanks with the appropriate day of the week.

"If today is ..., tomorrow is...."

1. Si aujourd'hui c'est lundi, demain c'est _____.
2. Si aujourd'hui c'est mercredi, demain c'est _____.
3. Si aujourd'hui c'est samedi, demain c'est _____.
4. Si aujourd'hui c'est mardi, demain c'est _____.
5. Si aujourd'hui c'est jeudi, demain c'est _____.
6. Si aujourd'hui c'est dimanche, demain c'est _____.
7. Si aujourd'hui c'est vendredi, demain c'est _____.

B. STUDY page 98, *Conversation 2* and the *Vocabulaire* on page 99. You will hear four statements about the days of the week of classes. If the statement is true, write *Vrai;* if the statement is false, write *Faux.*

1. _____   2. _____   3. _____   4. _____

IV. Topic: *L'école*

A. 1. FIRST STUDY basic questions about subjects studied, Aim IIIB, pages 99-102 and the *Vocabulaire* on page 104. Then answer the following questions with a complete sentence in French.

1. Qu'est-ce que tu étudies à l'école? _____

_____

2. Quel est ton sujet favori? _____

_____

3. Qui est ton professeur de mathématiques? _____

_____

4. Où est ton professeur de mathématiques? _____

_____

5. Combien d'élèves est-ce qu'il y a dans ta classe d'anglais? _____

_____

6. Comment est ta classe d'anglais? _____

_____

7. Quand est ton examen de français? _____

_____

8. Pourquoi est-ce que tu aimes ou que tu n'aimes pas la classe de français? _____

_____

CORRECTIVE, UNIT IV   NAME _____

IV: *L'école* (continued)

2. Your teacher or peer partner will ask you seven questions related to the subjects you study.

1. _____
2. _____
3. _____
4. _____
5. _____
6. _____
7. _____

B. Write the French question word for each of the following:

1.	Who? _____ ?	5.	What?	_____ ?
2.	When? _____ ?	6.	What? (Which one?)	_____ ?
3.	Where? _____ ?	7.	How many?	_____ ?
4.	Why? _____ ?	8.	What is ... like? (How is ...?)	_____ ?

In the following dialogue Peter asks Helen a few questions about her classes. Fill in the appropriate question word in each of Peter's questions.

1. **Pierre:** _____ tu étudies à l'école?
    Hélène: J'étudie l'anglais, le français, l'histoire et l'art.

2. **Pierre:** _____ est ton sujet favori?
    Hélène: Mon sujet favori est l'anglais.

3. **Pierre:** _____ est ton professeur d'anglais?
    Hélène: Mon professeur d'anglais est Melle Johnson.

4. **Pierre:** _____ est ta classe d'anglais?
    Hélène: Ma classe d'anglais est intéressante, bonne et difficile.

5. **Pierre:** _____ d'élèves dans ta classe?
    Hélène: Il y a trente et un élèves dans ma classe.

6. **Pierre:** _____ est ton professeur?
    Hélène: Elle est dans la salle de classes 315.

7. **Pierre:** _____ est ton examen?
    Hélène: Mon examen est mercredi prochain.

8. **Pierre:** Est-ce que tu aimes ta classe de français?
    Hélène: Oui, je l'aime.

9. **Pierre:** _____ est-ce que tu l'aimes?
    Hélène: J'aime la classe parce que le professeur enseigne bien et j'ai de bonnes notes.

CORRECTIVE, UNIT IV   NAME _____

V. Topic: *Un dialogue entre M. Durand et Melle Dupuis*

FIRST READ Aim IIB, page 89 *Exercice oral* A and B carefully. Then write an appropriate response in each blank.

1. **M. Durand:** Bonjour, Melle Dupuis. Comment allez-vous?

    Melle Dupuis: _____ . Et vous?

2. **M. Durand:** Je suis un peu fatigué aujourd'hui.

    Est-ce que vous travaillez beaucoup au collège?

    Melle Dupuis: Oui, _____ .

3. **M. Durand:** Où est-ce que vous étudiez?

    Melle Dupuis: _____ . *(at the library)*

4. **M. Durand:** Qu'est-ce que vous faites après le travail?

    Melle Dupuis: Après le travail je _____, _____ et _____.

5. **M. Durand:** A bientôt Melle Dupuis.

    Melle Dupuis: _____ , M. Durand.

VI. Topic: *Résumé de grammaire*

A. FIRST STUDY Aim IIC, page 94. What you have just read is a summary of the grammatical concept of "subject-verb agreement" as it applies to regular -ER verbs of the present tense.

B. Study the following explanation for the same concept:
    The **stem** of a verb is found by removing the -er from the infinitive (the dictionary form of the verb). Find and write the **stem** of each of the following infinitives.

    Example: écout**er** - écout

1. regarder- _____
3. nager- _____
5. chanter- _____

2. travailler- _____
4. étudier - _____
6. marcher- _____

When we use *"er"* verbs in sentences we **add** endings to the stem. The endings are different for each subject group. Review the **singular** subject pronouns and the ending that each one takes. Then, in the spaces at the right of each ending, write the correct form of the infinitive *"jouer"*.

Subject Pronouns	*Ending*	*Correct form* (stem + ending)
je	e	_____
tu	es	_____
il/elle	e	_____
nous	ons	_____
vous	ez	_____
ils/elles	ent	_____

CORRECTIVE, UNIT IV   NAME_____

    C. Now add the appropriate ending to each verb (or stem).

1. **Marie:** Est-ce que tu dans___ beaucoup dans les parties?
2. **Pierre:** Oui, je dans___ beaucoup dans les parties.
3. **Marie:** Est-ce que tu jou___ de la guitare aussi?
4. **Pierre:** Oui, je jou___ de la guitare et je chant___ aussi.

5. **Marie:** Est-ce que vous regard___ la télévision après le travail?
6. **Mme Dupont:** Oui, je regard___ la la télévision après le travail.
7. **Marie:** Où achet___-vous la nourriture?
8. **Mme Dupont:** J'achèt___ la nourriture au supermarché.

    D. Add the appropriate endings:

Madame Dupont voyag___ à Quimper pendant l'été. Elle voyag___ avec son mari. Monsieur Dupont nag___ dans l'océan Atlantique. Il march___ beaucoup durant les vacances parce qu'il travail___ beaucoup dans son bureau. Elle nag___ à la plage avec son mari.

    E. Write any appropriate **subject pronoun** in the blanks.

1. _____ chante très bien.

2. _____ parle peu au téléphone.

3. _____ étudie beaucoup à la maison.

4. _____ travaille avec Joseph.

5. _____ a de bonnes notes.

6. _____ réponds à beaucoup de questions.

ENRICHMENT, UNIT IV   NAME _____

I. *Squares* (Les carrés)

A. Squares #1: *L'école.* This game is similar to TIC-TAC-TOE. One player uses the circle "0" as his symbol, and the other player uses the "X". Each player first <u>states</u> and then <u>writes</u> the appropriate action in the blank. Players take turns.

Jean _____ le français.	L'élève _____ un examen.	Le professeur _____ la leçon.
La fille _____ beaucoup de questions	Marie _____ beaucoup à la maison.	Le garçon _____ une bonne note.
L'élève _____ une mauvaise note.	Le professeur _____ français très bien.	Claude_____ peu de questions.

B. Squares #2: *Le temps libre.* (Leisure time)

Il ne _____ la télévision.	Elle_____ à la discothèque.	_____ vous au tennis?
Madame Pottel _____ la nourriture lundi.	Monsieur Colin _____ à la maison après le travail.	Mademoiselle Conte n'a pas de voiture; elle _____ à l'école à pied.
Thérèse_____ très bien du piano.	Charles n' _____ pas la radio.	Mon ami _____ dans un supermarché après les classes.

II. *Qu'est-ce que tu fais...?* (What do you do...?)

Write three activities you do during the following time periods. Mention a minimum of nine different activities.

1. A l'école je _____, _____
   et _____.

2. Après les classes je _____,
   _____ et _____.

3. A la fin de la semaine je _____
   _____ et _____

4. Pendant les vacances d'été je _____
   _____ et _____.

5. Pendant les vacances de Noël je _____
   _____ et _____.

III. *Pour communiquer dans une langue...*

In order to communicate in a language, one needs to be able to carry out one of its principal functions, to get information. One of the best ways to obtain information is to employ question words, known formally as interrogative pronouns.

A. The following is a list of question words. **Write a question you have already learned** for each of the following. Remember what must be written before and after every question in French. Be sure you know the meaning of each of these words. Refer to page 104 *(Vocabulaire)* for any word whose meaning you are not sure of.

1. Qu'est-ce que ...? _____

2. Quel...? _____

3. Comment...? _____

4. Où...? _____

5. Quand...? _____

6. Combien ...? _____

7. Qui? _____

8. Pourquoi? _____

B. Read carefully the following **responses** to the questions asked; then **write the appropriate question word** (refer to A. above) which elicited each response in the blank space in each question.

1. _____ âge a Jean?
    Il a quatorze ans.

2. _____ le professeur?
    Elle est intelligente et sympathique.

3. _____ Est-ce qu'Annie achète la nourriture?
    Elle achète la nourriture au supermarché.

4. _____ est ton meilleur ami?
    Charle est mon meilleur ami.

5. _____ est-ce que M. Dupont marche?
    Il marche après le travail.

6. _____ Est-ce que Thérèse fait la cuisine?
    Elle fait très bien la cuisine.

7. _____ est-ce que Jean est fatigué?
    Il est fatigué parce qu'il travaille beaucoup.

8. _____ de langues est-ce que tu étudies?
    J'étudie l'espagnol et le français.

9. _____ est la capitale du Luxembourg?
    La capitale du Luxembourg est Luxembourg.

10. _____ est-ce que tu voyages en Suisse?
    Je voyage en Suisse pendant l'été.

11. _____ est-ce que vous nagez?
    Je nage dans l'océan Pacifique.

12. Avec_____ est-ce que tu danses beaucoup?
    Je danse beaucoup avec Marie.

13. _____ est-ce que tu joues au tennis?
    Je joue au tennis le dimanche.

14. _____ est-ce que tu aimes l'hiver?
    J'aime l'hiver parce que j'aime la neige
    et j'adore skier.

ENRICHMENT, UNIT IV   NAME _____

III. (continued)

C. Answer the following questions with a complete sentence in French.

1. Quand est-ce que tu étudies? _____

_____

2. Combien d'heures est-ce que tu étudies pour un examen? _____

_____

3. Dans quelles classes est-ce que tu as de bonnes notes? _____

_____

4. Dans quelles classes est-ce que tu as beaucoup de devoirs? _____

_____

5. Comment est-ce que ton professeur de français enseigne? _____

_____

6. Avec qui est-ce que tu parles français? _____

_____

7. Où est-ce que tu passes beaucoup d'examens? _____

_____

8. Est-ce que tu aimes l'école? Pourquoi? _____

_____

_____

D.   Mon temps libre *(My free time)*

1. Quels sports fais-tu? _____

_____

2. Est-ce que tu travailles après l'école? _____

_____

3. Est-ce que tu appartiens à une équipe *(team)* ? Quel club ou quelle équipe? _____

_____

4. Qu'est-ce que tu fais quand il fait beau? _____

_____

5. Qu'est-ce que tu fais lorsqu'il fait mauvais? _____

_____

6. Quel est ton jour favori de la semaine? Pourquoi? _____

_____

IV. *Une lettre à un correspondant (une correspondante)*

A. You have been given the opportunity to write to a French-speaking penpal. In the **first paragraph** tell him/her the following personal information. Write one sentence for each item.

1. First greet him/her
2. Introduce yourself
3. State where you are from (country)
4. State your age
5. State your birthday
6. State the year in which you were born
7. State where you live (city, etc.)
8. State your telephone number
9. State what you are like (six descriptive adjectives)
10. State five activities that you like to do

B. In the **second paragraph** tell him/her the following information related to school. Write one sentence for each item.

State:
11. what school you attend *("Je vais au lycée* [name].*")*
12. where the school is located
13. if you live near or far from the school (*près de*- near; *loin de*- far)
14. how you travel to school (*en train* - by train; *en autobus* - by bus;
      en voiture - by car; *à pied* - to walk)
15. all the subjects you are studying in school
16. what classes you have on Monday (in chronological order) and whether you have the same
      program every day
17. what your favorite class is and why
18. the name of your French teacher
19. how many students there are in your French class
20. what your class is like (two descriptive adjectives)
21. if you take a few or a lot of tests in the class
22. if you get good grades in class
23. when your next *(prochain)* test is
24. if you have a lot of homework in the class
25. if you like your French class (and why or why not)

C. In the **third paragraph** ask him/her five questions related to school and ask him/her what s/he likes to do after school, during the weekend and during the summer vacation. You can end your letter by using the very common farewell, *A bientôt,* and then sign your name.
Note: Write your letter on this page and finish on a sheet of your own paper.

_____, ____ _____ 19__
(ville)   (le jour) (mois)

Cher ami _____,
          ou
Chère amie _____,

_____

_____

_____

_____

_____

_____

_____

ENRICHMENT, UNIT IV   NAME_____

V. Lecture (Reading)

Read the paragraph and then answer each question which follows in a complete sentence in French.

Deux amis

1   Michel est un jeune homme qui a seize ans. Il regarde beaucoup la télévision après l'école. Il
2 écoute aussi la musique à la radio. Il fait toujours la cuisine parce que sa mère travaille le soir.
3 Après le repas Michel parle au téléphone tous les soirs. Il parle à son amie Hélène. C'est une
4 jeune fille de quinze ans. Hélène joue de la guitare tous les après-midi à la maison. Elle regarde
5 très peu la télévision parce qu'elle pratique la guitare. Aussi elle étudie beaucoup pour les
6 examens parce qu'elle aime avoir de bonnes notes. Hélène travaille beaucoup le samedi. Elle aide
7 sa mère à acheter la nourriture au supermarché et à nettoyer la maison. Le dimanche elle sort
8 avec son ami Michel.

Vocabulaire:

1   un jeune homme   *a young person*
2   le soir   *in the evening*
3   tous les soirs   *every evening*
4   tous les après-midi   *every afternoon*
6   aider   *to help*
7   nettoyer   *to clean*

Comprension de la lecture:

1. Quel âge a Michel?

_____

2. Quand est-ce qu'il écoute la musique?

_____

3. Pourquoi est-ce que Michel fait la cuisine?

_____

4. Avec qui est-ce qu'il parle au téléphone?

_____

5. Quel âge a son amie?

_____

6. Quand est-ce qu'Hélène joue de la guitare?

_____

7. Pourquoi est-ce qu'elle étudie beaucoup pour les examens?

_____

8. Où est-ce qu'Hélène et sa mère achètent la nourriture?

_____

9. Avec qui est-ce qu'elle sort le dimanche?

_____

ENRICHMENT, UNIT IV   NAME _____

VI. *Trouvez la personne...* (Find the person...)

You are going to interview several students in the class to find out information related to school, to after school and to weekend activities. The goal of this activity is to see who can get the most questions answered on this interview sheet. You will have about fifteen minutes. **Speak to only one person at a time.** Ask each person a specific question such as *"Est-ce que tu travailles après l'école?"* The person addressed must answer in a complete sentence: *"Après l'école je travaille,"* or *"Après l'école je ne travaille pas."* When you get a "yes" answer, write the person's name in the space provided and move on to another person. Use a person's name only once and find one person for each question on the sheet.

Trouvez la personne...

1. ...qui travaille après l'école. _____
2. ...qui va à l'école à pied. _____
3. ...qui n'aime pas la classe d'éducation physique. _____
4. ..qui n'a pas de bonnes notes en histoire. _____
5. ...pour qui la classe favorite est la science. _____
6. ...qui ne regarde pas la télévision. _____
7. ...qui est dans une classe qui a plus de trente élèves. _____
8. ...qui joue au basketball le dimanche. _____
9. ...qui est dans une classe qui a moins de douze élèleves. _____
10. ...qui a un examen la semaine prochaine. _____
11. ...pour qui la classe d'anglais est bonne et difficile. _____
12. ...qui fait bien la cuisine. _____
13. ..qui joue de la guitare à la fin de la semaine.

Vocabulaire:

5. pour qui   *whose / for whom*
7. plus de   *more than*
   Est-ce que tu es dans une classe qui...?   *Are you in a class that...?*
   Je suis dans...   *I'm in...*
   Je ne suis pas dans...   *I'm not in...*
9. moins de   *less than*
13. la fin de la semaine   *weekend*

SITUATIONS ORALES, UNIT IV   NAME _____

A. Function: Providing and Obtaining Information
Role: I am your parent.
Purpose: At the start of the school year I want to know about your program.
I will begin the conversation.

1. **Père/Mère:** Qu'est-ce que tu étudies à l'école cette année?
   Toi: _____.

2. **Père/Mère:** Quelle est ta classe favorite?
   Toi: _____.

3. **Père/Mère:** Comment est la classe?
   Toi: _____.

4. **Père/Mère:** Combien d'élèves est-ce qu'il y a dans la classe?
   Toi: _____.

5. **Père/Mère:** Dans quelle classe est-ce que tu as beaucoup de travail?
   Toi: _____.

B. Function: Expressing Feelings
Role: I am your friend.
Purpose: You want to tell me about your favorite class.
You will begin the conversation.

1. **Toi:** _____.
   Ami(e): Pourquoi est-ce que tu aimes la classe?

2. **Toi:** _____.
   Ami(e): Qui est le professeur?

3. **Toi:** _____.
   Ami(e): Comment est le professeur?

4. **Toi:** _____.
   Ami(e): Qu'est-ce que tu fais dans la classe?

5. **Toi:** _____.
   Ami(e): J'aime cette classe aussi.

C. Function: Providing and Obtaining Information
Role: I am your counselor.
Purpose: I want to know why you are getting poor grades in a particular class.
I will begin the conversation.

CORRECTIVE, UNIT V   NAME _____

I. TOPIC: *Deux familles françaises*

A. FIRST STUDY the relationships of members of a family, Aim I, page 118 *(Vocabulaire)*. Next study *Exercise orale 3,* pages 112-113 to check that you know how to read a French family tree.

B. Answer the questions which follow this French family tree.

```
         Marie Nédélec (née Dupuis)----------------------- Robert Nédélec
              (69 ans)                                          (76 ans)
         ┌──────────────────────────┐              ┌──────────────────────────┐
  Anne Nédélec---------- Jean Nédélec          Claire Nédélec---------- Paul Durant
    (38 ans)              (45 ans)               (47 ans)                 (53 ans)
   ┌───────────────────────────┐              ┌───────────────────────────┐
Françoise Nédélec      Pierre Nédélec       Philippe Durant        Laure Durant
   (21 ans)               (15 ans)             (24 ans)               (16 ans)
```

1. **Le mari** de Marie Nédélec s'appelle _____

2. **La fille** de Robert Nédélec s'appelle _____

3. **Le père** de Françoise Nédélec s'appelle _____

4. **La soeur** de Philippe Durand s'appelle _____

5. **Le grand-père** de Pierre Nédélec s'appelle _____

6. **La tante** de Laure Durant s'appelle _____

7. **Le cousin** de Philippe Durant s'appelle _____

8. **La nièce** de Claire Nédélec s'appelle _____

9. **Le petit-fils** de Robert Nédélec s'appelle _____

10. **Les parents** de Jean Nédélec et de Claire Nédélec s'appelent _____

_____

C. Now you make up the next set of relationships using the French family tree above.

11. Le frère de _____ s'appelle _____

12. La mère de _____ s'appelle _____

13. Le fils de _____ s'appelle _____

14. La grand-mère de _____ s'appelle _____

D. Your teacher or peer partner will ask you a few relationships to which you can respond orally or in writing.

II. TOPIC: *La famille de... / Quel âge a ...?*

A. FIRST REVIEW numbers 1-99, (Unit I, page 18, pages 25 and 31).

B. Next write the age **in French words** of each member of the French families in Topic I of this corrective.

1. Marie Nédélec a _____ ans.

2. Robert Nédélec a _____ ans.

3. Paul Durant a _____ ans..

4. Anne Nédélec a _____ ans.

5. Claire Nédélec a _____ ans.

6. Pierre Nédélec a _____ ans.

7. Philippe Durant a _____ ans.

8. Le frère de Robert Nédélec a _____ (81) ans.

9. La mère de Marie Nédélec a _____ (98) ans.

C. Your teacher or peer partner will state the **ages** of a few people. After the second repetition, write the age of each person in Arabic numbers.

1. _____   2. _____   3. _____   4._____   5. _____   6. _____

III. TOPIC: *Ma famille*

A. FIRST STUDY the basic family questions: Aim II, page 119, Aim III, page 120, Aim IV, page 122, Aim V, page 124, Aim VI, page 126, Aim VII, page 128 and Aim VIII, page 130.
B. The following are answers given by Joseph to the questions asked by his friend Jean. **Write the questions** asked by Jean.

1. **Jean:** _____?
    Joseph: Il y a six personnes dans ma famille.

2. **Jean:** _____?
    Joseph: Il y a ma mère, mon père, mes deux soeurs, mon frère et moi.

3. **Jean:** _____?
    Joseph: Mon frère s'appelle Tomas.

4. **Jean:** _____?
    Joseph: Mon père a quarante et un ans.

5. **Jean:** _____?
    Joseph: Ma mère est petite, mince, belle, bonne et sympatique.

6. **Jean:** _____?
    Joseph: Mon père est des Etats-Unis.

CORRECTIVE, UNIT V   **NAME** _____

III. (continued)

7. **Jean:** _____?
   Joseph: Ma soeur Anne étudie beaucoup, joue au tennis, danse beaucoup, va au cinéma, fait des exercises et fait bien la cuisine.

8. **Jean:** _____?
   Joseph: Mon frère et moi nous parlons beaucoup, nous allons au supermarché, nous lavons les assiettes, nous jouons au baseball, nous regardons la télévision et nous jouons de la guitare.

C. Answer the following questions about your family with a complete sentence in French.

1. Combien de personnes est-ce qu'il y a dans ta famille? _____

2. Qui sont-elles? _____

3. Comment s'appelle ton frère (ou ta soeur) (ou ton cousin ou ta cousine)? _____
   _____

4. Quel âge a ta mère (ou ton père)? _____

5. Comment est ta soeur (ou ta cousine)? _____

6. D'où est ton grand-père (ou grand-mère)? _____
   _____

7. Que fait ta mère (ou ton père)? *(trois activités)* _____
   _____

8. Que faites-vous toi et ton frère (ou ta soeur) (ou ta mère)? *(trois activités)* _____
   _____

D. Your teacher or peer partner will ask you a few questions about your family. Answer in complete sentences in French.

1. _____
2. _____
3. _____
4. _____
5. _____

CORRECTIVE, UNIT V   NAME _____

IV. TOPIC: *La famille de...*

A. FIRST STUDY the questions in Part III of this Corrective.

B. You meet a French-speaking peer at a party who recently arrived from Switzerland. What questions would you ask of him/her to find out the following about his/her family?

1. How many people there are in his/her family _____
    _____

2. The name of his/her sister _____

3. Where his/her grandfather is from _____
    _____

4. The age of his/her cousin (female) _____

5. What his/her brother is like _____
    _____

6. What his/her mother does _____
    _____

7. What he/she and his/her father do _____
    _____

ENRICHMENT, UNIT V   NAME _____

II. *L'arbre généalogique de ma famille*

A. Write in the **proper names** of your own family to make your family tree.

grand-père   grand-mère   grand-père   grand-mère

père   mère

moi frère   soeur   frère   soeur

B. Give the following information for each of the family members indicated in **complete sentences** in French:

  1. name   2. age   3. country of birth (where the person is from)
  4. four characteristics (what the person is like) 5. birthdate
  6. three activities each person does

A. **Ma mère**

  1. _____
  2. _____
  3. _____
  4. _____
  5. _____
  6. _____
  _____

B. **Mon frère (ou ma soeur);** si vous n'avez pas de frères et soeurs (**Mon cousin ou ma cousine**)

  1. _____
  2. _____
  3. _____
  4. _____
  5. _____
  6. _____
  _____

C. **Mon grand-père (ou ma grand-mère);** si vos grands-parents sont décédés (**Mon oncle ou ma tante**)

  1. _____
  2. _____
  3. _____
  4. _____
  5. _____
  6. _____
  _____

Vocabulaire: décédé   *dead, no longer living*

III. Carrés (Tic-Tac-Toe)

Write the **correct form** of any -ER verb to make a meaningful sentence. You can play the game with a peer partner or do the activity yourself.

A. Game #1

Nous _____ mal.	Monsieur Sandoux _____ à la maison.	_____ française?
Je/J' _____ beaucoup de questions	Mes amis _____ la radio.	La Maîtresse _____ la leçon.
Anne et Hélène _____ beaucoup au téléphone.	_____ vous en Suisse cet été?	Mon amie et moi _____ la télévision.

B. Game # 2

Vous _____ bonnes notes.	Robert _____ bien au tennis.	Nous _____ le cha-cha-cha et la mamba aux parties.
Tu _____ très bien la guitare.	Les élèves _____ beaucoup d'examens.	Madame Boris _____ la nourriture à la maison
Mademoiselle Langeais _____ la nourriture au supermarché.	Je/J' _____ dans la mer Méditerranée l'été.	Vous _____ beaucoup dans le parc au printemps.

ENRICHMENT, UNIT V   NAME_____

VI. *Trouvez la personne... (Find the person...)*

You are going to interview each other about one another's families. The goal of this activity is to see who can get the most questions answered on this interview sheet. You will have about 12 - 15 minutes. **Speak to only one person at a time.** Ask each person a specific question such as *Est-ce que tu as beaucoup de frères et soeurs?* The person addressed must answer in a complete sentence: *Oui, j'ai beaucoup de frères et soeurs,* or *Non, je n'ai pas beaucoup de frères et soeurs.* When you get a "yes" answer write the person's name only once and find one person for each question on the sheet.

Trouvez la personne...

1. _____ qui n'a ni frères ni soeurs.

2. _____ qui a une grande famille.

3. _____ dont la mère ou le père n'est pas des Etats-Unis.

4. _____ qui a un frère (ou une soeur) de quinze ans.

5. _____ qui a un frère (ou une soeur) qui est grand(e).

6. _____ qui a un frère qui s'appelle Robert (ou une soeur qui s'appelle Marie).

7. _____ qui a un frère (ou une soeur) qui joue de la guitare.

8. _____ qui a un frère (ou une soeur) qui parle beaucoup au téléphone.

9. _____ dont le grand-père (ou la grand-mère) parle français.

10. _____ qui va au cinéma avec un frère (ou une soeur).

Vocabulaire:

1. la personne qui ...   *the person* **who**
2. ni...ni...   *neither...nor...*
3. dont   *whose*

SITUATIONS ORALES, UNIT V   NAME _____

    A. Function: Socializing, Providing and Obtaining Information
      Roles: You are a foreign exchange student and I am the mother (father) of the host family.
      Purpose: We are socializing and you are going to tell me about your family.
        I will begin the conversation.

1. **Mère (père):** Combien de personnes y-a-t-il dans ta famille?

    L'élève: _____

2. **Mère (père):** Qui sont-elles?

    L'élève: _____

3. **Mère (père):** Comment s'appelle ta mère?

    L'élève: _____

4. **Mère (père):** D'où est-elle?

    L'élève: _____

5. **Mère (père):** Quelle âge a-t-elle?

    L'élève: _____

6. **Mère (père):** Comment est-elle?

    L'élève: _____

    B. Function: Expressing Feelings
      Roles: I'm your best friend.
      Purpose: You want to tell me how you feel about your brother or sister.
        You will begin the conversation by **stating his/her age.**

1. **Toi:** _____

    Meilleur ami(e): Comment est ton frère (ta soeur)?

2. **Toi:** _____

    Meilleur ami(e): Que fait-il (elle)?

3. **Toi:** _____

    Meilleur ami(e): Que faites-vous toi et ton frère (soeur)?

4. **Toi:** _____

    Meilleur ami(e): Que fait ton frère (ou ta soeur) que tu n'aimes pas?

5. **Toi:** _____

    Meilleur ami(e): Quel dommage!

Vocabulaire:
quand il/elle...   *when he/she...*
Quel dommage! *What a pity!*
ennuyer   *to bother, to annoy*
Cela m'ennuie *It bothers me*

    C. Function: Providing and Obtaining Information
      Roles: I am a new student in one of your classes.
      Purpose: You wish to find out about my family. You will begin the conversation.

ENRICHMENT, UNIT VII   NAME _____

I. Squares (Tic-Tac-Toe)

Write the **correct** form of any infinitive to make a **meaningful** sentence. You can play the game with a peer partner.

A. Game 1

Nous	Mon amie	Paul et Jean
_____	_____	_____
beaucoup de cadeaux.	trois miles.	en Floride.
J' _____ les fenêtres quand il fait chaud.	_____ tu de l'eau avec la nourriture?	Mon père _____ toujours le journal.
_____ -vous la leçon de français?	Joseph _____ beaucoup de lettres à ses amis.	Ma famille et moi _____ dans les restaurants.

B. Game 2

Ma mère	Je	Mes soeurs
_____	_____	_____
bien la cuisine.	toujours les ordures.	la vaisselle.
Mon petit frère _____ la table.	Mon père et mon frère _____ la maison.	_____ tu la nourriture au supermarché?
Ma famille _____ toujours à six heures et demie.	Mon frère ainé ne _____ rien à la maison.	Mon père et moi _____ beaucoup d'exercices.

C. Game 3: Make up your own game of "Squares" on your own paper. You may refer to the **activities** listed on pages 169-171. Use different subjects for each activity.

II.

FIRST STUDY the following forms of the irregular verb *"être"* in the present tense.

Je **suis** dans ma chambre.   Nous **sommes** à l'école.
Tu **es** à la bibliothèque.   Vous **êtes** au restaurant.
Il **est** au parc.   Ils **sont** à l'université.
Elle **est** à la partie.   Elles **sont** au cinéma.

We use this verb to state **the location** of someone (people) or something (things). State **eight** different hours of the day and the **place** where different people you know are. *Examples:*

Il est dix heures du matin. Je suis dans la classe d'art.
Il est une heure et quart de l'après-midi. Ma mère est dans la cafétéria du travail.

1. _____
2. _____
3. _____
4. _____
5. _____
6. _____
7. _____
8. _____

III.

FIRST STUDY the following forms of the irregular verb *"avoir"* in the present tense.

J'**ai** un ordinateur.   Nous **avons** un tourne-disque.
Tu **as** un vidéo.
Vouz **avez** un poste de radio.   Vous **avez** une voiture.
Il **a** une machine à écrire.   Ils **ont** une télévision.
Elle **a** une bicyclette.   Elles **ont** une machine à laver.

State eight different possessions that people you know have. Describe each possession using a different adjective. *Examples:*

Mes parents ont une voiture **neuve**.
Mon ami a une **belle** maison.
Ma soeur et moi nous avons un **bon** ordinateur.
J'ai un **petit** tourne disque.

1. _____
2. _____
3. _____
4. _____
5. _____
6. _____
7. _____
8. _____

IV.

State what is in your room (at least five of your possessions) and how each reflects your interests. Write a minimum of five complete sentences in French.

_____

_____

_____

_____

_____

_____

_____

V.

Read the following narration told by Marthe Duclos. The first time read to understand the general meaning. The second time read to find the answers to the questions which follow the narration.

1   Je m'appelle Marthe Duclos. J'ai trente-cinq ans. Je suis de Québec. J'habite dans la 74ème

2   rue à Manhattan dans la ville de New York. J'ai mon propre appartement que j'aime beaucoup. Je

3   suis secrétaire dans un bureau en ville.

4   Il y a cinq personnes dans ma famille: mes parents, mes deux soeurs et moi. Ma mère s'appelle

5   Marie. Elle a soixante-deux ans. Elle est petite, gentille et sympathique. Elle travaille beaucoup à

6   la maison. Mon père s'appelle Maurice et il a soixante-cinq ans. Il est petit, mince et très actif. Il

7   ne travaille plus; il est à la retraite. Il aime beaucoup faire de la marche et cultiver son jardin.

8   Mes parents vivent dans une maison en Californie.

9   Ma soeur Isabelle a trente-quatre ans. Elle est petite, grosse et généreuse. Elle est coiffeuse

10 et elle travaille trois jours par semaine. Elle aime faire de la marche et elle marche tous ses jours.

11 Elle est mariée et son mari s'appelle Pierre. Il est grand, beau et blond. Il est des Etats-Unis. Il

12 aime réparer les voitures. Ils vivent aussi dans une maison en Californie.

13   Ma jeune soeur s'appelle Laure. Elle a trente-trois ans. Elle est petite, mince et intelligente.

14 Elle est femme d'intérieur. Elle est mariée et elle a deux enfants: un fils et une fille. Son mari

15 s'appelle Michel. Il est grand, fort et athlète. Il est américain et il est programmeur d'ordinateurs.

16 Mon neveu Christian a quatre ans et ma nièce Nicole a deux ans. Ils habitent dans le Minnesota.

17 L'autre partie de la famille habite au Québec. Mon grand-père qui a quatre-vingt-dix ans est bon

18 et gentil. Il vit avec mes oncles dans une maison à la campagne. J'aime recevoir des lettres de lui.

19 Je lui écris aussi. J'ai beaucoup d'oncles et de cousins et quelquefois ils m'écrivent. J'aime

20 beaucoup recevoir des lettres de notre famille du Québec.

21   Nous sommes une famille très unie. Tous les dimanches je parle à mes parents au téléphone.

22 Mes soeurs aussi parlent avec eux. Tous les ans à Noël, ma soeur Laure, sa famille et moi, nous

23 voyageons en Californie pour voir mes parents et ma soeur Isabelle. Le jour de Noël mes parents

24 préparent un grand repas et nous nous réunissons tous autour de la grande table pour manger et

25 parler. Noël est le jour de fête favori de ma famille. Le meilleur cadeau de Noël pour nous, c'est

26 d'être ensemble et de partager.

ENRICHMENT, UNIT VII NAME _____

V. (continued)

Vocabulaire:

2. j'ai mon propre appartement   *my own apartment*
3. en ville   *downtown*
7. être à la retraite   *to be retired*
9. coiffeur, coiffeuse   *beautician*
10. par semaine   *per week*
11. elle est mariée   *she is married*
12. réparer   *to repair*
14. femme d'intérieur   *housewife*
15. américain(e)   *American*
17. l'autre partie   *other side*   mon grand-père qui   *my grandfather who*
18. à la campagne   *in the country*   j'aime   *I like, I love*
20. notre   *our*
21. une famille unie   *united*
22. tous les ans   *every year*
23. pour   *to, in order to*
24. un repas   *a meal*   nous nous réunissons   *we gather*
25. jour de fête   *holiday*   le meilleur cadeau   *the best present*
26. être ensemble et partager   *to be together and share*

Répondez aux questions avec une phrase complète en français. (*Answer the following questions about Martha's family with a complete sentence in French*)

1. D'où est Marthe? _____
2. Dans quelle ville est-ce qu'elle habite? _____
3. Avec qui est-ce qu'elle vit? _____
4. Combien de personnes est-ce qu'il y a dans la famille de Marthe? Qui sont-elles? _____
   _____
   _____
5. Quel âge a la mère de Marthe? _____
6. Est-ce que le père de Marthe travaille? _____
7. Dans quel état vivent les parents de Marthe? _____
8. Comment est Isabelle, la soeur de Marthe? _____
9. Qu'est-ce qu'Isabelle aime faire? _____
10. Comment s'appelle la jeune soeur de Marthe? _____
11. Est-ce qu'elle est mariée? Combien a-t-elle d'enfants? _____
    _____
12. D'où est le mari de Laure? _____
13. Où habitent le grand-père et beaucoup d'oncles et cousins de Marthe? _____
    _____

ENRICHMENT, UNIT VII   NAME _____

V. (continued)

14. Quand est-ce que Marthe parle à ses parents au téléphone? _____

_____

15. Pourquoi est-ce que Marthe et Isabelle et sa fille vont en Californie? _____

_____

16. Qui prépare un grand repas le jour de Noël? _____

_____

17. Quel est le jour de fête favori de la famille de Marthe? _____

_____

VI.

Read the following narration told by Martha's father. After the second reading answer the questions which follow.

1   Je m'appelle Vincent Duclos. J'habite dans une maison privée dans une petite ville a

2   soixante miles à l'est de Los Angeles. La ville est petite mais elle a un très grand centre

3   commercial avec toutes sortes de magasins. Dans la ville il y a quelques bâtiments publiques tels

4   que l'hôpital, une bibliothèque, une poste, un commisariat de police, une caserne de

5   pompiers et plusieurs écoles publiques. Il y a aussi quelques endroits pour s'amuser, des cinémas,

6   des restaurants et des discothèques. Mon quartier est tranquille sans le bruit ni la circulation des

7   grandes villes comme Los Angeles. Mes voisins sont sympathiques et aimables et nous nous

8   aidons quand c'est néccésaire.

9   J'aime beaucoup ma maison. Il ya sept pièces dans ma maison. Il y a: deux chambres, la salle

10   de séjour, la salle à manger la cuisine et les deux sallse de bain. Les chambres sont grandes et

11   confortables. Chaque chambre a un très grand placard et une large fenêtre par où entre beaucoup

12   de lumière. Ma femme aime beaucoup la cuisine parce qu'elle est moderne et elle a tout. Le soir

13   nous passons beaucoup de temps dans la salle de séjour où nous regardons la télévision et nous

14   parlons avec nos amis que nous voyons souvent. La salle à manger est belle mais petite.

15   Ma femme et moi nous faisons beaucoup de choses à la maison. L'été j'aime faire la cuisine sur

16   le barbecue qui est sur la terrasse de la maison. Le dimanche nous invitons toujours nos amis à

17   déjeuner avec nous. Ce que j'aime le plus dans la maison, c'est le jardin où je passe beaucoup de

18   temps.

19   Comme en Californie il fait beau presque toute l'année, je cultive des fleurs et des légumes

20   dans mon jardin. Ma femme passe beaucoup de temps dans le jardin au printemps quand il ne fait

21   pas trop chaud. L'été, elle préfère être à l'intérieur de la maison. Elle aime tricoter, faire la cuisine

22   et nettoyer la maison. Je suis à la retraite, mais j'aime rester actif. Je vais avec ma femme faire

23   les courses, je nettoie les fenêtres, je répare ma voiture et d'autres choses à la maison. Nous

24   sommes très contents dans notre maison.

ENRICHMENT, UNIT VII   NAME _____

VI. (continued)

Vocabulaire:

1. la ville   *a town*   une petite ville   *a small town*
2. mile   *mile*   à l'est   *to the east*   un centre commercial   *a shopping center*
3. toutes sortes de magasins   *all kinds of stores*   bâtiments publiques   *public buildings*
4. la poste   *post office*   la caserne de pompiers   *fire station*
    le commisariat de police   *police station*
5. un endroit pour s'amuser   *place of recreation*
6. le quartier   *neighborhood*   sans   *without*   le bruit   *noise*   ni   *nor*
7. comme   *like*   le voisin   *neighbors*   aimable   *kind*
    nous nous aidons   *we help each other*
8. quand c'est nécéssaire   *it is necessary*
11. (une armoire) un placard   *a closet*   grand, spacieux   *ample, spacious*
    par où entre beaucoup de lumière   *through which enters ... light*
14. que nous voyons souvent   *who visit us frequently*
16. le barbecue   *barbecue*
17. ce que j'aime le plus   *that which I like most*
19. presque   *almost*   toute l'année   *the whole year*   cultiver   *to cultivate*
21. être à la maison   *to be at home*   tricoter   *to knit*
22. rester actif   *to keep active*
23. d'autres choses   *other things*

Répondez aux questions par une phrase complète en français.

1. Où habite Vincent Duclos? _____

    _____

2. Est-ce qu'il y a beaucoup ou peu de magasins dans le centre commercial de la ville? _____

    _____

3. Quels services publiques est-ce qu'il y a dans la ville? _____

    _____

4. Et quels endroits pour s'amuser est-ce qu'il y a dans la ville? _____

    _____

5. Comment est la petite ville où habite Vincent? (**deux** caractéristiques) _____

    _____

6. Quelles sont les pièces de sa maison? _____

    _____

7. Quelle pièce est-ce que sa femme aime le plus? Pourquoi? _____

    _____

8. Quelles activités est-ce que Vincent et sa femme font dans la salle de séjour? _____

    _____

9. Comment est la salle à manger de la maison? _____

    _____

10. Quand est-ce que Vincent fait la cuisine sur le barbecue? _____

    _____

ENRICHMENT, UNIT VII   **NAME** _____

VI. (continued)

11. Où passe-t-il beaucoup de temps? _____

    _____

12. Qu'est-ce qu'il cultive? _____

13. Qu'est-ce que la femme de Vincent aime faire? _____

    _____

14. Est-ce que Vincent travaille ou est-il à la retraite? _____

15. Que fait-il pour rester actif? _____

    _____

VII.

You can refurnish any room in your home. List what you will buy.

Je veux meubler ...   *I want to refurnish...*   Je veux acheter...   *I want to buy...*

1. _____   4. _____

2. _____   5. _____

3. _____   6. _____

VIII.

You have an opportunity to create your "dream house". On your own paper, describe its size, its rooms, the furniture and appliances in each room, the exterior of the house, and so forth. Use complete sentences in French. You may wish to include a floor plan.

ENRICHMENT, UNIT VII

NAME _____

IX. *Petites annonces*

A common source for those who want to rent or buy apartments in Paris is the daily newspaper *le Monde*. Read the list of apartments available for rent and then decide which advertisement (ad) you would answer given the different reasons for looking for particular apartments.

appartements ventes

PRIX INTÉRESSANT
MAISON 4 P.
Mᵒ ST-GEORGES. Cuis., bns.
Bon état, cour privative.
Calme. Soleil, 16, r. Navarin
Sam., dim. 14 h à 17 h.

1

16ᵉ arrdt
BD MURAT
Partic. vd dans petit imm.
ancien. Faibles charges.
BEAU 2 P. 42 m²
R-de-ch. s/jardins et cour.
Living 21 m² + chb. 14 m².
Petite cuis. équip., s. de bns.
REFAIT NEUF. TRÈS CALME
950 000 F. 42-80-16-23
ou 47-70-09-56

2

STUDIO A PARIS, à LOUER EN AOÛT
(au mois ou semaine) quartier marais
(place des Vosges) grand et meublé,
belle vue, 2000FF semaine ou 6500 FF/
mois. Tél: 011.33.1.34.69.84.96. Mme
Bailly.

3

2ᵉ arrdt
Mᵒ BOURSE
BEAU STUDIO. Cuis.
S/rue. Poutres. Charme.
Cuis., tt cft. Rangements.
520 000 F. 48-04-84-48

4

---

locations non meublées offres

Paris
STUDIO A LOUER
angle Réaumur-Sébastopol
48-57-53-29 (après 17 heures)

5

14ᵉ arrdt
AV. DU MAINE
Imm. récent. 3 P. 65 m².
1ᵉ ét. Asc. Clair. Bon état.
Gardien, code. Particulier.
Prix : 1 450 000 F
Tél. : 43-22-25-66

6

3ᵉ arrdt
MARAIS ARCHIVES NTLES
Mᵒ RAMBUTEAU. Imm. classé.
BEAU 2 P. 3ᵉ ét. asc. Cuis. Tt cft,
moulures, cheminée, cave.
840 000. 48-04-84-48

7

7ᵉ arrdt
QUAI VOLTAIRE
Part. vend beau studio
35 m². Calme, sur cour. Cuisine américaine, s.d.bns.
T. 42-61-28-12, à part. 19 h 30

8

---

1. If you want to buy a studio in the 7e with a "cuisine américaine" answer ad # _____.

2. If you want to buy a house "en bon état" at a good price, answer ad # _____.

3. If you want to live in an "Immeuble classé" and buy an apartment with a chimney, answer ad # _____.

4. If you want to rent a studio in Paris in August answer ad # _____.

5. If you want to live in an "Immeuble récent" with a guard, answer ad # _____.

6. If you want to rent a studio with furniture, answer ad # _____.

7. If you want to live near the subway station "Bourse" answer ad # _____.

8. If you want to buy an apartment totally redone and quiet, answer ad # _____.

ENRICHMENT, UNIT VII   NAME _____

X. *Rencontrez la personne qui ...*

You are going to interview each other to find others in the class who fit the following categories related to the topic "House and Home". The goal of this activity is to see who can get the most questions answered in about fifteen minutes. Speak to only one person at a time. Ask each person a specific question such as *"Est-ce que tu vis dans un appartement?"* The person addressed must answer in a complete sentence: *"Oui, je vis dans un appartement"*, or *"Non, je ne vis pas dans un appartement"*. When you get a **yes** answer write the person's name in the space provided and move on to another person. Use a person's name only once and find one person for each question on the sheet.

Recontrez la personne...

1. ...qui vit dans un immeuble de plus de six etages. _____

2. ...qui met la table tous les jours. _____

3. ...dont la salle de bain est moyenne et belle. _____

4. ...qui fait ses devoirs dans la salle à manger. _____

5. ...dont le frère sort les ordures. _____

6. ...qui a plus de six pièces dans sa maison ou son appartement. _____

7. ...qui lave la vaisselle après le repas. _____

8. ...dont la famille passe beaucoup de temps dans la salle de séjour. _____

9. ...qui vit au deuxième étage de son immeuble ou sa maison. _____

10. ...dont l'immeuble ou la maison a un jardin. _____

11. ...qui nettoie sa chambre à la fin de la semaine. _____

12. ...dont la soeur lave ses vêtements. _____

13. ...qui prend un bain le matin. _____

14. ...dont la mère (dont le père) fait. _____

15. ...qui aide beaucoup ses frères. _____

Vocabulaire: vivre *(irregular): to live*

je vis	nous vivons
tu vis	vous vivez
il/elle vit	ils/elles vivent

1. de plus de...   *of more than*
3. dont...   *whose...*
11. à la fin de la semaine   *during the weekend*
13. le matin   *in the morning*

SITUATIONS ORALES, UNIT VII   NAME _____

A. **Function:** Providing and Obtaining Information
   Role: I am your friend.
   Purpose: You have recently moved to a new home and I want to find out about it.
      I will begin the conversation.

1. **Ami(e):** Depuis quand *(how long)* est-ce que tu habites dans la maison?

   Toi: _____

2. **Ami(e):** Quelle est ton adresse?

   Toi: _____

3. **Ami(e):** Combien de pièces est-ce qu'il y a dans ta maison?

   Toi: _____

4. **Ami(e):** Dans quelle pièce est-ce que tu passes beaucoup de temps?

   Toi: _____

5. **Ami(e):** Comment est ta maison?

   Toi: _____

6. **Ami(e):** Pourquoi est-ce que tu aimes ta nouvelle maison?

   Toi: _____

B. **Function:** Socializing
   Role: I am a French teenager you meet on vacation in Paris.
   Purpose: I want to know about your home and the responsibilities of the members of
      your family. I will begin the conversation.

1. **Un(e) jeune:** Où est-ce que tu habites?

   Toi: _____

2. **Un(e) jeune:** Est-ce que tu habites dans une maison ou un appartement?

   Toi: _____

3. **Un(e) jeune:** A quel étage est-ce que tu habites?

   Toi: _____

4. **Un(e) jeune:** Combien de pièces est-ce qu'il y a dans ta maison?

   Toi: _____

5. **Un(e) jeune:** Quelle est ta pièce favorite?

   Toi: _____

6. **Un(e) jeune:** Pourquoi?

   Toi: _____

7. **Un(e) jeune:** Qui fait la cuisine et qui fait la vaisselle?

   Toi: _____

8. **Un(e) jeune:** Comment est-ce que tu aides à la maison?

   Toi: _____

SITUATIONS ORALES, UNIT VII   NAME _____

C. **Function:** Providing and Obtaining Information
   Role: I am your friend. You have just moved to another house or apartment.
   Purpose: I call you on the telephone to find out about your new place. I will begin.

D. **Function:** Expressing Feelings
   Role: I am your friend and you are visiting me in my new house or apartment.
   Purpose: Tell me your opinion about it. You will begin the conversation.

E. **Function:** Persuasion
   Role: I am your parent and the family is looking for a new home.
   Purpose: Try to persuade me to buy one of the houses we have seen.
      You will begin the conversation.

Notes

CORRECTIVE, UNIT VIII   NAME_____

I. Topic: *Qu'est-ce qui fait mal...?*

A. FIRST STUDY the parts of the body, Aim IA, pages 187-189 and the *Vocabulaire,* page 190.

B. Next pretend you are the person in the picture. **First state** what part of the body hurts you and then write this statement in the space provided.

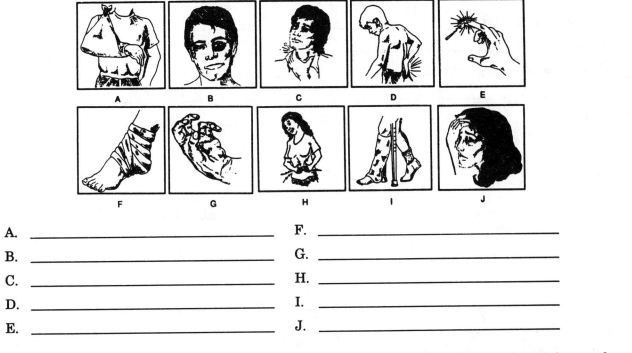

A. _____   F. _____

B. _____   G. _____

C. _____   H. _____

D. _____   I. _____

E. _____   J. _____

C. Your teacher or peer partner will state what part of the body hurts a few of the people above. After the second repetition, choose the letter which corresponds to what you hear.

1.____   2.____   3.____   4.____   5.____   6.____

II. Topic: *La réponse adéquate*

A. Read the dialogues on pages 202, 205 and 207 and study the *Vocabulaire* on pages 206 and 208.

B. Next write the **English meaning** of each of the following frequently used communicative expressions.

1. Bonjour! Quoi de neuf? _____

2. Comme je suis content de te voir! _____

3. Moi aussi. _____

4. Est-ce que tu voudrais (aimerais)? _____

5. Je voudrais. / Non je ne voudrais pas. _____

6. Toi ... très bien. _____

7. Je suis content(e) ravi(e)... _____

CORRECTIVE, UNIT VIII   NAME _____

II. (continued)

8. Pourquoi est-ce que tu ne peux pas? _____

9. C'est bien. _____

10. Je ne sais pas. _____

11. Ne n'ai pas ma montre. _____

12. à tes souhaits. _____

13. Au revoir / A bientôt. _____

14. Je ne peux pas. _____

15. Ça va / malade / fatigué(e). _____

16. Je vous en prie. _____

17. Bonjour. _____

18. Je n'ai pas le temps. _____

19. Bonne idée. _____

C. Choose **one or more** appropriate responses given for each of the following statements or questions from Part **B** above.

1. Bonjour! Quoi de neuf? _____

2. Merci. _____

3. (Someone sneezes.) _____

4. Bonjour. _____

5. Comme je suis content(e) de te voir! _____

6. Est-ce que tu voudrais aller à la discothèque? _____

7. Tu parles très bien français. _____

8. Veux-tu que je t'appelle? _____

9. Quelle heure est-il? _____

10. A bientôt. _____

III. Topic: *Un note rapide*

A. FIRST STUDY pages 191 - 197.

B. Tomorrow is the day of your French test and you do not feel well today. Write a note to your teacher telling him/her in three complete sentences: a) you are sick and you have a headache, b) you **also** have a fever and your throat hurts you, and c) you are not going to school tomorrow; you're going to the doctor.

Cher(chère) professeur _____,

_____

_____

_____

_____

IV. Topic: *La santé*

A. FIRST STUDY the *Vocabulaire,* pages 190 and 193. Then read the dialogues of Aim IC, page 194.

B. Next fill in the appropriate expression in each of the blanks.

A.

Anne: Bonjour Pierre. _____ ?

Pierre: Je suis fatigué. Et _____ ?

Anne: Je ne vais pas bien.

Pierre: _____ ?

Anne: J'ai mal à l'estomac et à la tête.

Pierre: _____.

_____ vite!

Anne: _____.

Pierre: Pourquoi est-ce que tu ne vas

pas chez toi?

Anne: Bonne idée. A bientôt, Pierre.

Pierre: _____, Anne.

B.

M. Dupont: Bonjour, Mme Vial.

_____ ?

Mme Vial: Ça va, merci. Et _____ ?

M. Dupont: Pas très bien.

Mme Vial: _____ ?

M. Dupont: J'ai un rhume et j'ai mal à l'oreille.

Mme Vial: _____

_____ vite!

M. Dupont: _____.

Mme Vial: Pourquoi est-ce que vous n'allez

pas voir le docteur?

M. Dupont: Vous avez raison. Je vais voir

le docteur demain.

_____, Mme Vial.

Mme Vial: Au revoir, M. Dupont.

V. Topic: *Une annonce médicale*

What number would you call if you had trouble with your teeth? Circle the correct letter.

Dr. Philippe HENDEL
Ancien stagiaire du Dr. TESSIER
(Hopital Foch à Paris)
Associate Professor University of
New Jersey and Roosevelt
Hospital
Chirurgie plastique
Chirurgie de la main
Chirurgie craniofaciale
425W. 59ème rue,6ème étage
(212) 582-1772
sur rendez-vous

Dr. Sylvie Epelbaum
Dermatologie
Diplômée Faculté de médecine
de Paris et de New York
Maladies de la peau
et du cuir chevelu
traitement des rides,varices
injections de collagène.
104 East 40th street
between Park & Lexington Avenue
(212) 861-3600

Dr C. MAMOURIS
NEUROLOGIE, PSYCHIATRIE
Maladies des nerfs; émotionnelles mentales;
dépression
insomnie; maux de tête;
Faculté de médecine Paris et N.Y.
936 Fifth Ave.New York, NY 10021
(212) 744-1181

Olivier Nicolay
DDS - MMSC
Orthodontie
sur rendez-vous
30 E 60 ème rue
Ste. 1504
(212) 319-9777

A. 744-1181

B. 319-9777

C. 582-1772

D. 525-6399

CORRECTIVE, UNIT VIII   NAME _____

VI. Topic: *Les passe-temps*

A. FIRST STUDY Aim IIB, *Les sports,* pages 200-201 and read Aim III, pages 202, 207 and 209 and the *Vocabulaire* that follows each reading.

B. Answer the following questions about your hobbies and other leisure time activities with a complete sentence in French.

1. Est-ce que tu aimes faire du sport? _____
    _____

2. A quels sports est-ce que tu joues? _____
    _____

3. Quel est ton sport favori? _____

4. Quand est-ce que tu joues à ton sport favori? _____
    _____

5. Est-ce que tu voudrais jouer au basket dimanche prochain? (Oui) _____
    _____

6. Avec qui est-ce que tu veux jouer? _____

7. Est-ce que tu participes à quelques activités après les classes? Auxquelles? ou pourquoi non?
    _____
    _____

8. Où est-ce que tu vas pendant les vacances? (summer) _____
    _____

9. Où est-ce que tu vas pendant les vacances de Noël? (Christmas) _____
    _____

10. Quand est-ce que tu sors avec tes amis? (State 2-3 time periods.) _____
    _____
    _____

CORRECTIVE, UNIT VIII   NAME _____

VII. Topic: *Mes activités à la fin de la semaine*

Review pages 198 - 206 if you have not done so already. Then answer the following questions with a complete sentence in French and state the weekend time period during which you do each activity.
Example: Je vais au parc **le samedi après midi.**

1. Est-ce que tu vas faire des achats? _____

2. Est-ce que tu vas au cinéma ou à une discothèque? _____
_____

3. Est-ce que tu fais du sport? _____

4. Est-ce que tu sors avec tes amis? _____
_____

5. Est-ce que tu joues d'un instrument de musique? Lequel? _____
_____

6. Est-ce que tu regardes les sports à la télévision? Lesquels? _____
_____

7. Est-ce que tu vas à l'église (au temple)(à la synagogue)? _____
_____

8. Est-ce que tu étudies pour les examens? _____
_____

9. Est-ce que tu travailles? Où? _____
_____

ENRICHMENT, UNIT VIII

NAME _____

I. Les parties du corps

Find **sixteen** French names for parts of the body. Circle each word and then write it with its appropriate definite article (*le, la*) in the spaces provided.

```
T A D O S U V E M B N G O P
E Y E Z J M U R S R T O U I
T H N B A L M E R A U R V E
E S T O M A C W U S O G C D
A F D U B I O E I L V E H O
G B H C E J U K B A E Z E I
E N C H A Q Z M A I N L V G
R E T E L M O P C G K U E T
S Z U N U E B O D I L M U O
O R E I L L E O H Y E U X Z
```

1. _____   5. _____   9. _____   13. _____
2. _____   6. _____   10. _____   14. _____
3. _____   7. _____   11. _____   15. _____
4. _____   8. _____   12. _____   16. _____

II.

Write a short note to a friend refusing an invitation from him/her because of health reasons. Your note should consist of at least three complete sentences in French.

_____ le _____ 19 __

Cher(e) ami(e), _____ ,

_____

_____

_____

_____

_____

Je t'embrasse,

_____

ENRICHMENT, UNIT VIII   NAME _____

III. *Une visite chez le docteur*

Fill in the appropriate expression in each of the blanks.

C'est vendredi après-midi. Marie recontre son ami Paul qui est malade. Marie lui recommande d'aller chez le docteur.

1. **Marie:** Bonjour! _____ ?

2. **Paul:** Je ne vais pas bien.

3. **Marie:** _____ ?

4. **Paul:** Jai _____ et jai mal _____.

5. **Marie:** Je suis navrée _____!

    Pourquoi est-ce que tu ne _____ pas chez le docteur?

6. **Paul:** Bonne idée. Je _____ appeler le docteur maintenant pour prendre rendez-vous..

    Paul appelle le docteur au téléphone.

7. **Receptioniste:** _____ ! _____ Allô?

8. **Paul:** _____, Paul Dupont. Je veux _____ voir le docteur demain.

9. **Receptioniste:** Est-ce que ça va à trois heures?

10. **Paul:** Oui, _____.

    C'est Samedi. Paul arrive à trois heures, pour la consultation avec le docteur.

11. **Receptioniste:** Bonjour, Paul.

12. **Paul:** Bonjour, Melle Durand. _____?

13. **Receptioniste:** Très bien, merci. Assieds-toi s'il te plaît.

14. **Docteur:** Paul, entre.

15. **Paul:** Je suis _____!

    Le docteur examine Paul et lui pose des questions.

16. **Docteur:** Paul, combien d'examens est ce-que tu as la semaine prochaine?

17. **Paul:** _____ quatre, docteur.

18. **Docteur:** Paul, tu _____ bien. Est-ce que tu es nerveux?

19. **Paul:** Oui, docteur. Je _____ très nerveux quand _____ beaucoup d'examens.

20. **Docteur:** Ne t'inquiète pas *(don't worry)* et etudie beaucoup. Bonne chance! *(...luck)*, Paul.

21. **Paul:** Merci _____, docteur.

ENRICHMENT, UNIT VIII   NAME _____

IV.

FIRST STUDY the following forms of the irregular verb *"aller"* in the present tense.

Je **vais** à la maison de mon ami.	Nous **allons** à la bibliothèque
Tu **vas** au cinéma.	Vous **allez** à la discothèque.
Il/Elle **va** à l'église	Ils/Elles **vont** au magasin.

State eight different places to which people you know go to and the general time period in which they go there. ***Examples:***

Mes amis vont au match de football **dimanche matin.**
Je vais à la bibliothèque **après les classes.**
Mon amie et moi, nous allons dans les magasins **à la fin de la semaine.**
Melle Rousseau va au travail **tous les jours.**

1. _____
2. _____
3. _____
4. _____
5. _____
6. _____
7. _____
8. _____

V.

Read the following narration told by Jean Perrigaud in which this French teenager tells you about his school life and some of his leisure time activities.

1   Je m'appelle Jean Perrigaud. Je suis de France. Je suis né à Tours, une très jolie ville qui est
2   à 150 km a l'ouest de Paris. Cela fait six ans que je vis dans la capitale dans la rue de Chartres
3   avec mes parents, mes deux soeurs et mon frère. J'ai dix-sept ans. Mon anniversaire est le 15
4   juin. Je vais à la même école que Pierre mon meilleur ami et Thérèse, mon amie d'Amérique du
5   nord. L'école s'appelle le lycée Emile Zola. J'étudie la littérature et la langue française, les
6   sciences, l'anglais, l'histoire et les mathématiques. Ma classe favorite c'est les sciences. J'aime les
7   sciences parceque mon professeur enseigne bien et j'aimerais être docteur. La classe est toujours
8   intéressante et j'aime apprendre tout ce que je peux. Il y a 3 examens et un examen final. Géné-
9   ralement les examens sont difficiles, mais j'étudie beaucoup pour les passer avec une bonne note.
10   Le lundi et le mercredi, avant les classes, j'étudie avec Pierre. Il m'aide avec les mathématiques et
11   je l'aide avec les sciences.
12   J'étudie aussi avec Thérèse le jeudi après les classes. L'autre classe que j'aime beaucoup, c'est
13   l'anglais. L'anglais est une langue très difficile. Thérèse m'aide avec la prononciation de l'anglais.
14   La classe est très grande et il y a peu d'opportunités de practiquer beaucoup dans la classe. Le
15   mardi et le jeudi pendant le déjeuner Thérèse et moi nous allons à la cafétéria pour manger. Là,
16   nous parlons, j'ai l'opportunité de pratiquer l'anglais et j'apprends beaucoup. Je veux aller en
17   Angleterre pendant les grandes vacances pour visiter et améliorer mon anglais. Après les classes
18   je vais à la bibliothèque et je fais mes devoirs. Généralement, j'y passe quatre heures parceque
19   j'ai beaucoup à lire pour mes classes. A sept heures et demie, Pierre termine son travail et je le
20   rencontre dans notre cafétéria favorite pour bavarder. Souvant Thérèse vient aussi. Nous parlons
21   de tout: de l'école, des sports, des amis et de nos plans pour le future.
22   A la fin de la semaine, je fais beaucoup de choses différentes. Le samedi matin je joue au
23   football avec un groupe d'amis de l'école. A une heure je vais à la maison manger avec ma famille.
24   L'après-midi après le déjeuner je rencontre encore mes amis. Nous faisons une promenade et nous
25   allons au cinéma ou à la discothèque. Le dimanche, j'étudie pour mes examens à la maison. Jaime
26   aussi regarder un match de football à la télévision et écouter de la musique. Je suis content de
27   mes études et de mes activités à la fin de la semaine.

Vocabulaire:

2. le kilomètre (km)   *kilometer*
4. le/la même   *same*
5. la langue française   *French language*
7. enseigner   *to teach*   j'aimerais être   *I want to be*   le docteur   *doctor*
8. tout ce que je peux   *all that I can*   généralement   *generally*
9. pour les passer   *In order to pass them*
10. avant   *before*   Il m'aide   *He helps me*
11. je l'aide   *I help him / her*
15. pendant le déjeuner   *at lunch time*
17. Angleterre   *England*   pendant   *during*   améliorer   *to improve*
19. terminer   *to finish*
20. recontrer   *to meet*   notre   *our*   bavarder   *to chat*
    venir   *to come* Je viens, elle vient
21. de tout   *all*
24. encore   *again*   faire une promenade   *to take a walk*

ENRICHMENT, UNIT VIII   NAME _____

V. (continued)

Questions: Repondez aux questions avec une phrase complète en français.

1. D'où est Jean Perrigaud? _____

2. Où est Tours? _____

3. Avec qui est-ce qu'il vit? _____

4. Comment s'appelle le meilleur ami de Jean? _____

5. Qui est Thérèse? _____

6. Quelle est la classe favorite de Jean? Pourquoi? _____
_____

7. Combien d'examens est-ce qu'il y a par an? _____
_____

8. Pourquoi est-ce qu'il étudie beaucoup pour les examens? _____
_____

9. Quand est-ce Jean étudie avec Pierre? _____
_____

10. Est-ce que l'anglais est une langue facile ou difficile? _____

11. Est-ce qu'il y a peu ou beaucoup d'élèves dans la classe d'anglais? _____
_____

12. Où est-ce que Jean et Thérèse parlent anglais? _____
_____

13. Quand est-ce que Jean veut aller en Angleterre? _____
_____

14. Combien d'heures est-ce qu'il passe à la bibliothèque après les classes? _____
_____

15. Où est-ce que Jean, Pierre et Thérèse bavardent souvent? _____
_____

16. De quoi (about what) parlent les trois amis? _____
_____

17. Que fait Jean le samedi matin? _____
_____

18. A quelle heure est-ce qu'il va à la maison déjeuner avec sa famille? _____
_____

19. Où vont Jean et ses amis le samedi après-midi? _____
_____

20. Que fait Jean le dimanche? _____
_____

ENRICHMENT, UNIT VIII   **NAME** _____

VI.

Read the following page of *L'Officiel des spectacles* and then answer the questions that follow.

L'OFFICIEL DES SPECTACLES
du mercredi 29 juillet au mardi 4 aout 1992

*Les informations que nous publions nous son communiquées par les organisateurs
sous réserve de chamgements de dernière minute.*

L'OFFICIEL DES SPECTACLES. - - Cette semaine: 1, rue de Berri, angle 100, Champs-Elysées, 75008 Paris.
Téléphone: Rédaction: 45.62.70.64. Abonnement (payable d'avance), 1 an: 300F

A TRAVERS PARIS _____ 87	ENVIRONS	
Activités sportives _____ 87	Cinémas _____ 35	
Monuments-promenades _____ 89	Restaurants _____ 105	
Environs _____ 78	Concerts _____ 23	
MUSEES _____ 25	TELEVISION _____ 16	
RESTAURANTS _____ 93	THEATRES	
Spécialites _____ 94	Cafés-théatres _____ 14	
Fêtes et réceptions _____ 98	Programmes des théatres _____ 15	

Répondez aux questions: (circle your answer).

1. *L'Officiel des spectacles* is: A. a travel brochure.   C. the yellow pages.
                                     B. an entertainment guide.   D. an advertisement.

2. For which date would this work have helpful information?
     A. December 9   B. July 28   C. November 3   D. August 3

3. This work is published for the inhabitants of
     A. Lausanne, Switzerland   B. Antwerp, Belgium
     C. Paris, France   D. Montreal, Quebec

On what page would you find information about:

4. films in the movies? _____

5. museums? _____

6. concerts? _____

7. exhibits? _____

8. theater times? _____

ENRICHMENT, UNIT VIII   NAME _____

VII. *Jeu de la découverte*

1. Each partner will write six activities s/he most likes to do chosen from the list below.

2. Partners will take turns asking their opponent *Est-ce que tu aimes...?*

3. Partners will answer according to what they have written on their papers: *Oui, j'aime...* or *Non, je n'aime pas...*

4. The partner who asks the question will write his/her partner's *Oui* or *Non* in the space on the sheet next to the appropriate activity.

5. When one partner has guessed all six of the other's answers, that partner wins the game.

Choose six activities you like to do from the list below.

1. J'aime _____   4. J'aime _____

2. J'aime _____   5. J'aime _____

3. J'aime _____   6. J'aime _____

Oui or *Non* is to be recorded before each activity according to your partner's answers:

_____ jouer de la guitare	_____ monter à cheval
_____ skier	_____ aller à la plage
_____ jouer au tennis	_____ lire
_____ faire la cuisine	_____ regarder la télévision
_____ faire de la bicyclette	_____ courir
_____ nager	_____ écrire des lettres
_____ patiner sur la glace	_____ aller aux parties
_____ aller au cinéma	_____ écouter la musique
_____ chanter	_____ voyager
_____ manger	_____ danser
_____ travailler	_____ jouer au ballon
_____ parler au téléphone	

Vocabulaire:

monter à cheval   *to ride horseback*
patiner   *to skate*
     patiner sur la glace   *to iceskate*
nulle part   *nowhere, anywhere*

ENRICHMENT, UNIT VIII   NAME _____

VIII. *Mes pensées et mes sentiments*

Complete each of the following sentences to express your thoughts and feelings.

1.   Je n'ai pas le temps de (pour) _____

2.   J'ai toujours le temps de (pour)_____

3.   L'année prochaine je veux _____

4.   Je ne peux pas _____

5.   Je peux _____

6.   J'aime _____

7.   Je n'aime pas _____

8.   J'aimerais _____

9.   Je suis nerveux (se) quand je _____

10. Quand je suis malade _____

11. Je ne vais nulle part quand _____

12. Quand j'ai besoin d'argent je _____

13. Je suis content(e) quand je _____

SITUATIONS ORALES, UNIT VIII   NAME_____

    A. Function: Expressing Feelings
        Roles: I am your friend.
        Purpose: We are discussing the merits of various sports. You will begin by telling which sport is your favorite.

1. **Toi:** _____

    Ami(e): Pourquoi est-ce que c'est ton sport favori?

2. **Toi:** _____

    Ami(e): Quand est-ce que tu joues...?

3. **Toi:** _____

    Ami(e): Où est-ce que tu joues...?

4. **Toi:** _____

    Ami(e): Avec qui est-ce que tu joues...?

5. **Toi:** _____

    Ami(e): J'aime ce sport aussi.

    B. Function: Socializing
        Roles: I am a teenager your age and we have just met at a party.
        Purpose: I want to find out if we have the same interests. I will begin the conversation.

1. **Un(e) jeune:** Qu'est-ce que tu aimes faire pendant ton temps libre?
    Toi: _____

2. **Un(e) jeune:** Qu'est-ce que tu aimes mieux ... ou ...?
    Toi: _____

3. **Un(e) jeune:** Qu'est-ce que tu fais à la fin de la semaine?
    Toi: _____

4. **Un(e) jeune:** Avec qui...?
    Toi: _____

5. **Un(e) jeune:** Où est-ce que tu vas pendant les grandes vacances?
    Toi: _____

6. **Un(e) jeune:** J'y vais aussi.

    C. Function: Socializing
        Roles: I am your friend. I have been very sick and you are visiting me.
        Purpose: You start the conversation by finding out how I feel. Then you can tell me what is going on.

    D. Function: Providing and Obtaining Information
        Roles: I am your doctor and you are my patient.
        Purpose: You come to my office because you're not feeling well. I will begin.

    E. Function: Persuasion
        Roles: We are friends discussing plans for the weekend.
        Purpose: Convince me to go to a particular place this weekend. You begin by telling me where you want to go.

CORRECTIVE, UNIT IX   NAME _____

I. TOPIC: *La nourriture et la boisson*

A. FIRST STUDY pages 213 - 223, Aim IA - ID.
B. Then write next to each of the following foods and drinks the category to which each belongs. The five categories to choose from are *la viande, les légumes, les fruits, les desserts, les boissons.*

1. la saucisse chaude _____
2. la laitue _____
3. l'eau _____
4. le veau _____
5. Le maïs _____
6. l'omelette _____
7. les fraises _____
8. le jus d'orange _____
9. le mouton _____
10. le chocolat chaud _____

11. le lait _____
12. la carotte _____
13. la côtelette de porc _____
14. la glace _____
15. la tarte _____
16. les haricots verts _____
17. le soda _____
18. le poulet _____
19. le raisin _____
20. le jambon _____

C. Your teacher or peer partner will state five foods/drinks. After the second repetition, write the category to which each food or drink belongs.

1. _____ 2. _____ 3. _____ 4. _____ 5. _____

II. TOPIC: *Le couvert*

A. FIRST STUDY Aim V, pages 232 - 234. Next, write in a complete sentence the one item you are missing in each place setting as if you were seated at the table.

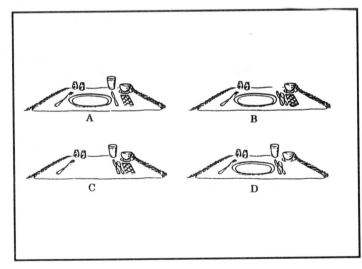

A. _____

B. _____

C. _____

D. _____

B. Your teacher or peer partner will state that one item of the place setting is missing. After the second repetition write the **letter** which corresponds to what you hear.

1. _____ 2. _____ 3. _____ 4. _____

CORRECTIVE, UNIT IX   NAME_____

III. TOPIC: *La réponse adéquate*

A. FIRST READ the *Lecture, Partie I* and *Partie II* of Aim VIA, pages 235 - 237 and the *Lecture, Partie I* and *Partie II* of Aim VIB, pages 239 - 241. Then review the *Vocabulaire* of each part.

B. Next write the English meaning of each of the following frequently used communicative expressions in French.

1. Cela fait longtemps que je ne t'ai pas vu. _____

   _____

2. Je suis fatigué(e) d'étudier. _____

3. Je ne sais pas. _____

4. Je n'ai pas ma montre. _____

5. C'est l'heure de manger. _____

6. Pourquoi est-ce que tu ne manges pas avec nous? _____

   _____

7. C'est bien. _____

8. J'aimerais. _____

9. Je te présente mon ami(e). _____

   _____

10. Enchanté(e). _____

11. Entrons. _____

12. Sortons. _____

13. Où sont les toilettes? _____

14. à droite _____

15. à gauche _____

16. Bon appétit! _____

17. Vous de même, vous aussi _____

18. Ecoute! _____

19. Je suis navré(e). _____

20. Qu'est-ce que tu penses ...? _____

CORRECTIVE, UNIT IX   NAME_____

C. Write **two appropriate responses** to each of the questions or statements which follow.

1. **Charles:** Quelle heure est-il?

   Monique: _____

   Antoine: _____

2. **Paul:** C'est l'heure de manger.

   Catherine: _____

   Philippe: _____

3. **Jean:** Joseph, j'aimerais te présenter mon ami Robert.

   Joseph: _____

   Robert: _____

4. **Claudine:** Pourquoi est-ce que tu ne manges pas avec nous?

   Thérèse: _____

   Rachelle: _____

5. **Barbara:** Où sont les toilettes?

   Rose: _____

   Louis: _____

6. **Marie:** Comment est la nourriture?

   Raoul: _____

   Hélène: _____

CORRECTIVE, UNIT IX · NAME_____

IV. TOPIC: *La nourriture et les boissons*

A. FIRST STUDY Aim II, pp. 224 - 227, Aim III, pp. 228 - 229 and Aim IV, pp. 229 - 231.
B. Then answer each of the following questions with **your own answer** after reading how another person has responded.

1. **Melle Cordier:** Est-ce que vous avez faim?
   M. Martin: Non, je n'ai pas faim.
   Vous: _____

2. **Anne:** Est-ce que tu as soif?
   Joseph: Oui, j'ai très soif.
   Toi: _____

3. **Melle Cordier:** Qu'est-ce que vous mangez quand vous avez faim?
   M. Martin: Quand j'ai faim, je mange un sandwich au fromage.
   Vous: _____
   _____

4. **Anne:** Qu'est-ce que tu bois quand tu as soif?
   Joseph: Quand j'ai soif je bois de l'eau.
   Toi: _____
   _____

5. **Melle Cordier:** Qu'est-ce que vous aimez mieux, le poisson grillé ou le poulet grillé?
   M. Martin: J'aime mieux le poisson grillé.
   Vous: _____

6. **Anne:** Qu'est-ce que tu aimes mieux, la pomme ou la poire?
   Joseph: J'aime mieux la poire.
   Toi: _____

7. **Melle Cordier:** Qu'est-ce que vous aimez mieux, le veau ou le bifteck?
   M. Martin: Je préfère le veau.
   Vous: _____

8. **Anne:** Qu'est-ce que tu préfères, le pudding ou la glace?
   Joseph: Je préfère le pudding.
   Toi: _____

9. **Melle Cordier:** Qu'est-ce que vous mangez pour le déjeuner?
   M. Martin: Pour le déjeuner je mange un sandwich au thon.
   Vous: _____

10. **Anne:** Qu'est-ce que tu manges pour le dîner?
    Joseph: Pour le dîner je mange du veau avec des haricots verts.
    Toi: _____

11. **Melle Cordier:** Quel est votre dessert favori?
    M. Martin: Mon dessert favoir est la tarte aux pommes.
    Vous: _____

12. **Anne:** Quelle est ta soupe favorite?
    Joseph: Ma soupe favorite est la soupe de légumes.
    Toi: _____

CORRECTIVE, UNIT IX   **NAME** _____

13. **Melle Cordier:** A quelle heure est-ce que vous prenez votre déjeuner?

 M. Martin: Je prends le déjeuner à une heure et quart.

 Vous: _____

14. **Anne:** A quelle heure est-ce que tu prends le dîner?

 Joseph: Je prends le dîner à sept heures et demie.

 Toi: _____

15. **Melle Cordier:** Avec qui est-ce que vous prenez le petit déjeuner?

 M. Martin: Je prends le petit déjeuner seule.

 Vous: _____

16. **Anne:** Avec qui est-ce que tu prends le déjeuner?

 Joseph: Je prends le déjeuner avec mon ami Paul.

 Toi: _____

17. **Melle Cordier:** Où est-ce que vous prenez le déjeuner?

 M. Martin: Je prends le déjeuner dans la cafétéria du travail.

 Vous: _____

 _____

18. **Anne:** Où est-ce que tu prends le dîner?

 Joseph: Je prends le dîner dans la salle à manger.

 Toi: _____

CORRECTIVE, UNIT IX   NAME_____

V. TOPIC: *Dans un restaurant français*

A. FIRST READ the menu on page 244 carefully.

B. Next answer the following questions about the menu in English.

1. How many francs does the Tartare steak cost? _____
2. What is the most expensive dessert? _____
3. How many kinds of soups are served? _____
4. How much does the "Salade de fruits" cost? _____
5. What is the most expensive hors d'oeuvre? _____
6. How much does an omelette with salmon fumé cost? _____
7. How are the fusilli served? _____
8. What is the most expensive drink? _____
9. How many kinds of desserts can you order? _____

VI. TOPIC: *Combien coûte?*

A. FIRST STUDY the numbers in Aim VIII, pp. 245 - 246.

B. Next fill in the blank with the cost of each dish of the menu on page 244
in French words.

1. La salade verte coûte _____ francs.
2. L'omelette au fromage coûte _____ francs.
3. La sole grillée coûte _____ francs.
4. Le veau aux champignons coûte _____ francs.
5. Le mouton aux haricots coûte _____ francs.
6. La tarte aux pommes coûte _____ francs.
7. La pêche melba coûte _____ francs.
8. Les hors d'oeuvres variés coûtent _____ francs.

I. *Puzle* (Wordsearch)

A. Write the French equivalent for each of the following foods and beverages.

B. Then see how many of these French foods and drinks you can find in the block of letters below. Circle each one that you find.

1. butter _____   11. fish _____
2. pudding _____   12. potatoes_____
3. tuna fish _____   13. ice cream _____
4. salad _____   14. bread _____
5. milk _____   15. carrot _____
6. cereal _____   16. lamb _____
7. cheese _____   17. grapes_____
8. eggs _____   18. soup _____
9. ham _____   19. hamburger _____
10. cake _____   20. pie_____

```
B O J A M B O N S T A S B
U T A R T E A L R Z Q M M
A L R U V U M A A L L O E
M N X V S R W I M C N U R
S T S C A R O T T E R T N
U V O L L E A F O R T O N
C O U Z A B G E M E B N Z
O D P U D D I N G A E Q R
N H E R E S O J L L C S A
F R O M A G E Z A E F L I
I F J U T A U N C M D H S
T H O N L T F O E L G J I
U X Y V O E S Q P P A I N
R W P Q K A P O I S S O N
E H A M B U R G E R K R S
```

ENRICHMENT, UNIT IX   NAME _____

II.

You have decided to open a restaurant serving both French and American food in the city in which you are living. Create a menu in French giving a variety of choices for each category given. Then write the price you would charge for each item in dollars and cents under the column labeled *prix* (price). Write the name of your restaurant in the blank. You may consult a French dictionary.

*RESTAURANT*_____

Soupes (3)   **Prix**   **Légumes (4)**   **Prix**

_____   _____   _____   _____

_____   _____   _____   _____

_____   _____   _____   _____

                                             _____   _____

Viandes et Poulet (5)   **Prix**

_____   _____   **Dessert (4)**   **Prix**

_____   _____   _____   _____

_____   _____   _____   _____

_____   _____   _____   _____

_____   _____   _____   _____

Poisson (2)   **Prix**   **Boissons (3)**   **Prix**

_____   _____   _____   _____

_____   _____   _____   _____

                                             _____   _____

Menu du jour # 1   **Prix**   **Menu du jour # 2**   **Prix**

_____   _____   _____   _____

_____   _____   _____   _____

_____   _____   _____   _____

_____   _____   _____   _____

ENRICHMENT, UNIT IX   NAME_____

III.

Make up dinner menus in French for the following people. Each menu must have three foods and a beverage.

#1. une personne qui **aime** manger   *(loves to...)*
#2. une personne qui **est au régime**   *(is on a diet)*
#3. un **végétarien(ne)**   *(a vegetarian)*
#4. un athlète   *(an athlete)*
#5. un Français
#6. un Américain

Menu 1

_____
_____
_____
_____

Menu 4

_____
_____
_____
_____

Menu 2

_____
_____
_____
_____

Menu 5

_____
_____
_____
_____

Menu 3

_____
_____
_____
_____

Menu 6

_____
_____
_____
_____

ENRICHMENT, UNIT IX NAME _____

IV. Carrés (Tic-Tac-Toe)

A. Game One: Write any food or drink to make a meaningful sentence.

J'aime manger le pain avec _____.	Pour le dessert j'aime le plus _____.	Quand il fait chaud je bois _____.
Quand il fait froid je bois _____ _____.	Pour le petit déjeuner je mange _____ _____.	Mon légume favori est _____.
Mon fruit favori est _____.	J'aime un sandwich au _____.	Dans un restaurant je préfère manger _____.

B. Game two: Write the appropriate part of the place setting.

Ma grand-mère sert la nourriture dans _____.	Mme Vautrin mange le poisson avec _____.	Garçon, il me manque le sel et _____.
Michel boit un soda dans un _____.	Ma mère met un _____ sur la table.	Paul mange les céréales avec une _____.
Melle Martin s'essuie avec une _____.	Rose coupe le poulet avec un _____.	M. Rodiez boit le thé dans une _____.

Vocabulaire:

la mappe	tablecloth	je m'essuie	nous nous essuyons
s'essuyer	to clean oneself	tu t'essuies	vous vous essuyez
		il/elle s'essuie	ils/elles s'essuient

ENRICHMENT, UNIT IX   NAME_____

V.

Read the following story and dialogue carefully **two times.** In the first reading, try to understand the general meaning. The second time, read to find the answers to the questions that follow.

1   C'est aujourd'hui vendredi 19 mai. Charles, un garçon de quinze ans, est très content.

2 Pourquoi? Il y a beaucoup de raisons. Demain matin, il n'y a pas de classes et il va à une partie le

3 soir. Il aime beaucoup danser. Il a beaucoup d'amies et elles veulent toutes danser avec lui dans

4 les parties. Il joue aussi très bien de la guitare et tout le monde aime chanter quand il joue.

5   Charles est un jeune qui habite à Paris, la capitale de la France. De lundi à mercredi, il va au

6 lycée Jean-Jacques Rousseau. Le jeudi il n'a pas de classes, mais vendredi et samedi matin il a

7 des cours. Il est très bon élève et il a de bonnes notes parce qu'il étudie beaucoup. Il veut être

8 avocat. Quand il a du temps libre, il joue au football et il lit beaucoup de livres. Il écrit aussi

9 beaucoup de lettres et de cartes postales à ses amis qui vivent dans d'autres régions de France.

10 Aujourd'hui, il recoit une lettre d'un de ses meilleurs amis Joseph.

11   Charles ouvre la lettre et la lit rapidement. Quand il lit la lettre, il est très content. Joseph

12 vient le voir demain pour deux jours. Ainsi les deux bons amis vont aller à la partie ensemble.

13   Dimanche, c'est l'anniversaire de Charles. Il recoit toujours beaucoup de cadeaux pour son

14 anniversaire. Toute sa famille, ses parents, ses grands-parents, ses deux soeurs, son frère et

15 Joseph vont dans un grand restaurant pour célébrer. Pour y arriver, ils voyagent dix minutes

16 en voiture. Le restaurant s'appelle "l'Aurée du Bois." Il est à la porte Maillot à l'entrée du Bois de

17 Boulogne. Ils entrent tous au restaurant à une heure de l'après-midi et ils s'asseyent à une très

18 grande table réservée par le père.

19 **Le père:** Qu'est-ce que nous allons manger? On dit que tout est très bon ici.

20 **Le grand-père:** Il y a beaucoup de monde au restaurant aujourd'hui.

21 **Garçon:** Aujourd'hui et tous les jours. Cela fait 20 ans que je travaille ici et tout le monde a

22 son plat favori. Qu'est-ce que vous voulez pour commencer?

23 **Charles:** Pour commencer je veux la quiche qui est mon entrée favorite. Je vais voir si elle

24 est aussi bonne que celle que fait ma mère.

25 **Garçon:** Et ensuite?

26 **Charles:** Ensuite je veux le veau aux champignons.

27 **Garçon:** Qu'est-ce que vous buvez?

28 **Charles:** Un coca-cola. Pour le dessert je prends la mousse au chocolat.

29   Le reste de la famille et Joseph demandent au garçon leurs plats favoris. Ils y passent

30 deux heures. Ils mangent tous très bien et il sont très satisfaits.

31 **Le père:** Garçon, l'addition, s'il vous plaît?

32 **Garçon:** Oui, monsieur.

33   Tout le monde sort du restaurant content et décide de marcher jusqu'à l'Arc de Triomphe

34 qui n'est pas loin du restaurant. Il fait beau, Charles et Joseph parlent du bon repas qu'ils

35 viennent de manger, de leurs équipes de football favorites et de leurs plans pour l'été.

Vocabulaire:

2. la raison   *the reason*

4. tout le monde   *everybody*

ENRICHMENT, UNIT IX   NAME_____

Vocabulaire: (cont.)

5. de ... a   *from ... to*
9. cartes postales   *postcards*
    d'autres régions   *other regions*
11. ouvrir   *to open*
    il la lit   *he reads it*
12. vient le voir   *is coming to visit*
    ensemble   *together*
13. le cadeau   *the gift*
15. pour y arriver   *to arrive there*
16. en voiture   *by car*
    l'entrée   *the entrance*
17. ils entrent tous   *they all come in (enter)*
    ils s'asseyent   *they sit down*

20. il y a beaucoup de monde   *there are many people*
24. aussi bonne que   *as good as*
26. le champignon   *mushroom*
30. être satisfait   *to be satisfied*
33. être content   *to be happy*
35. ils viennent de manger   *they just ate*

A. *Vrai ou Faux.* If the statement is true, write *Vrai*. If the statement is false, write *Faux* and correct the bold part of the statement

1. Charles va à une partie **vendredi.**   1. _____
2. Il **chante** beaucoup dans les parties.   2. _____
3. Il a de **mauvaises** notes à l'école.   3. _____
4. Il vit dans la capitale de **France.**   4. _____
5. Il veut être **docteur.**   5. _____
6. Charles aime **écrire des lettres.**   6. _____
7. Joseph passe **la fin de la semaine** avec
    Charles.   7. _____
8. Joseph et toute la famille vont à
    une partie pour célébrer l'anniversaire
    de Charles.   8. _____

B. Répondez aux questions avec une phrase complète en français.

1. Quel âge a Charles? _____
   _____
2. Avec qui est-ce qu'il danse aux parties? _____
   _____
3. Où vit Charles? _____
   _____
4. Pourquoi est-ce qu'il a de bonnes notes à l'école? _____
   _____
5. Que fait Charles pendant son temps libre? _____
   _____

ENRICHMENT, UNIT IX   NAME_____

6. De qui *(from whom)* est-ce qu'il reçoit beaucoup de lettres? _____

_____

7. Pourquoi est-ce que Charles est content? _____

_____

8. Quand est son anniversaire? _____

_____

9. Combien de personnes est-ce qu'il y a dans la famille de Charles? Qui sont-elles?

_____

_____

10. Comment vont-ils au restaurant? _____

_____

11. A quelle heure est-ce qu'ils entrent au restaurant? _____

_____

12. Comment est la nourriture au restaurant? _____

_____

13. Est-ce qu'il y a beaucoup ou peu de personnes au restaurant? _____

_____

14. Quelle est l'entrée favorite de Charles? _____

_____

15. Qu'est-ce qu'il prend pour le dessert? _____

_____

16. Que boit Charles? _____

_____

17. Combien d'heures est-ce qu'ils passent tous au restaurant? _____

_____

18. Qu'est-ce qu'ils décident de faire quand ils sortent du restaurant? _____

_____

19. Quel temps fait-il le dimanche 21 mai? _____

_____

20. De quoi *(about what)* parlent Charles et Joseph? _____

_____

ENRICHMENT, UNIT IX   NAME _____

VI. *Les recettes* (Recipes)

Here are the recipes of two typical dishes of France. You may wish to try one or both! Answer the questions which follow each recipe.

1. *La quiche Lorraine:* An old-time favorite for all occasions to be served hot or cold.

Ingrédients:

1 pâte à tarte congelée
2 tasses de fromage râpé (gruyère ou cheddar)
2 oeufs
1 tasse de crème fraîche
1/2 livre (250 grammes) de jambon

Préparation:

1. Faites chauffer le four à 350°.
2. Etalez 1 tasse de fromage râpé au fond de la pâte.
3. Coupez le jambon en petits morceaux et étalez le sur le fromage.
4. Battez la crème et les oeufs et versez-les sur le jambon.
5. Recouvez le tout avec la 2e tasse de fromage et mettez au four bien chaud.
6. Faites cuire pendant 30 à 35 minutes.

Vocabulaire:

la pâte à tarte congelée   *frozen pie crust*
fromage râpé   *shredded cheese*
la crème fraîche   *fresh cream*
1/2 livre   *1/2 lb*   250 gr   *250 grams*
faire chauffer le four   *to heat the oven*
étaler   *to spread*   étaler sur   *spread over*
le fond   *the bottom*
couper le jambon   *to cut the ham*
petits morceaux   *small pieces*
battre   *to beat*
verser   *to pour over*
recouvrir   *cover*   le tout   *everything*
mettre au four   *put in the oven*
faire cuire   *cook*

Answer the following questions in English:

1.   What kind of cheese can you use in this recipe? _____

2.   How many eggs does this recipe call for? _____

3.   How do you cut the ham?_____

ENRICHMENT, UNIT IX   **NAME** _____

2. ***Mousse au Chocolat:*** A very popular dessert among French people, particularly children. There is no cooking necessary.

Les ingrédients:

4 blancs d'oeufs
100 grammes de sucre en poudre
1/2 verre de crème fraîche
75 grammes de chocolat en tablette à cuire

Préparation:

1. Faîtes fondre à feu doux le chocolat dans 3 cuillères d'eau (ne pas le faire cuire).
2. Battez les jaunes d'oeufs, ajoutez le sucre, le chocolat, la crème fraîche.
3. Battez les blancs d'oeufs en neige très ferme.
4. Incorporez le mélange doucement.
5. Versez dans un compotier.
6. Mettez au réfrigérateur et servez frais.

Vocabulaire:

blancs d'oeufs   *egg whites*
sucre en poudre   *powdered sugar*
1/2 verre   *1/2 glass*
crème fraîche   *fresh cream*
feu doux   *low flame*
cuillère d'eau   *spoon full of water (soup spoon)*
battre les jaunes   *to beat the whites*
neige très ferme   *like firm snow*
incorporer   *to incorporate*
le mélange   *the mixture*
doucement   *slowly*
verser   *to pour*
un compotier   *a deep bowl (usually glass)*
servir frais   *serve cold*

Answer the questions in English:

1. What is the principal ingredient of *mousse au chocolat?* _____
   _____

2. What are the ingredients that you beat to make it a "mousse"? _____
   _____

114

ENRICHMENT, UNIT IX   NAME _____

VII. *Une lettre à un(e) correspondante*

You receive a letter from your French-speaking penpal asking you to tell him/her about your eating habits. Write a letter to him/her in which you give the following information. Begin your letter by greeting your penpal, asking him/her how the family is and then state how you and your family are. After this introduction write the following paragraphs (A, B, C, and D).

A. *Le petit déjeuner à la fin de la semaine*
1. Tell at what time you eat breakfast
2. Tell where you eat breakfast
3. Tell with whom you eat
4. Tell who prepares this meal
5. Tell what you eat for breakfast
6. Tell if you have time to eat breakfast before school

B. *Le déjeuner à l'école*
7. Tell at what time you eat lunch
8. Tell where you eat lunch
9. Tell why you like or don't like to eat there
10. Tell with whom you eat
11. Tell if you buy or bring your lunch
12. Tell what you eat for lunch

C. *Un dîner au restaurant ou dans un self service*
13. Tell at what time you eat an evening meal in either a restaurant or fast food establishment
14. Tell the name of the place where you eat supper out
15. Tell with whom you eat
16. Tell what you eat
17. Tell how much this meal usually costs
18. Tell if you leave a tip

D. *Ask your penpal five questions about his/her eating habits.*

Use the following format to indicate your city, the date, the salutation and the farewell. Write the letter on your own paper.

le _____, _____ 19 ___
(ville)

Cher ami (chère amie) _____,

_____

_____

_____

à bientôt,

_____

ENRICHMENT, UNIT IX   **NAME** _____

VIII. *Les réclames de restaurants américains à Paris*

After examining the advertisement on the following page, answer these questions.

1. Combien de Chicken McNuggets est-ce qu'on sert par boîte chez McDonald?

    A. 20   B. 12   C. 4   D. 18

2. Combien de parfums de "Shake" est-ce qu'on peut acheter?

    A. 1   B. 4   C. 3   D. 6

3. Combien de sauces est-ce qu'il y a dans les salades composées?

    A. 2   B. 4   C. 6   D. 5

4. Pour qui est le "Happy Meal"? _____

5. Est-ce que chez McDonalds on ne sert que du boeuf et du poulet?

    _____

116

Bon... appétit!

LES BOISSONS
CHAUDES ET FROIDES

LES FRITES
3 tailles : normale,
moyenne et grande

LE SHAKE
3 parfums : fraise,
chocolat et vanille

LES 4 SALADES COMPOSÉES
Jardin, Chef, Crevettes et Poulet,
avec 5 sauces au choix*

LE FILET-O-FISH

LE DOUBLE
CHEESEBURGER

LE CHEESEBURGER

LES CHICKEN McNUGGETS
Par boîte de 6, 9 ou 20, avec 4 sauces au choix**

LE HAPPY MEAL
Le menu des enfants

**Barbecue, chinoise, curry, moutarde.

Happy Meal, Filet-O-Fish, sont la propriété de McDonald's Corporation.

LE SUNDAE
3 nappages : fraise,
chocolat et caramel

LE BIG MAC

ROYAL ET
ROYAL CHEESE

LES CHAUSSONS AUX FRUITS

LE HAMBURGER

*Vinaigrette, vinaigrette légère, cocktail, fines herbes, fromage bleu.

Les noms suivants : Big Mac, Royal, Royal Cheese, Chicken McNuggets,

SITUATIONS ORALES, UNIT IX   NAME _____

A. Function: Persuasion
Roles: We are friends.
Purpose: You want to convince me to go to a particular place to eat. I will begin.

1. **Ami(e):** Allons manger. Où est-ce que tu veux aller?

   Toi: _____

2. **Ami(e):** Pourquoi est-ce que tu aimes ce restaurant?

   Toi: _____

3. **Ami(e):** Comment est la nourriture?

   Toi: _____

4. **Ami(e):** Quelle est ta nourriture favorite dans ce restaurant?

   Toi: _____

5. **Ami(e):** Combien coûte la nourriture?

   Toi: _____

6. **Ami(e):** Où est ce restaurant?

   Toi: _____

A. Function: Socializing
Roles: You are a new student in my school.
Purpose: You want to find out about lunch at school. You will begin the conversation by introducing yourself.

1. **Toi:** _____

   Moi: Je m'appelle ...

2. **Toi:** _____

   Moi: Je déjeune à midi et demie.

3. **Toi:** _____

   Moi: Je déjeune dans la cafétéria.

4. **Toi:** _____

   Moi: Je déjeune avec mes amis.

5. **Toi:** _____

   Moi: J'aime le plus le hamburger avec les frites.

6. **Toi:** _____

   Moi: Oui, j'aimerais manger avec toi aujourd'hui.

SITUATIONS ORALES, UNIT IX   NAME _____

C. Function: Providing and Obtaining Information
   Roles: You are a diner in a French restaurant and I am your waiter/waitress.
   Purpose: You wish to order dinner. You will begin by getting my attention.

D. Function: Expressing Feelings
   Roles: I am your French-speaking friend whom you have invited to dinner.
   Purpose: Ask me about my preferences in food and beverages so you can decide what to serve. You will begin the conversation.

E. Function: Persuasion
   Roles: I am your mother and you are my teenage son/daughter.
   Purpose: Convince me to take you out to eat this weekend. I will begin the conversation.

CORRECTIVE, UNIT X   NAME _____

I. Topic: *Les vêtements*

A. **FIRST STUDY** Aim I, page 251, Aim II, page 254 and *Vocabulaire,* page 256.

B. **Then write the name of each article of clothing or accessory next to the corresponding letter.**

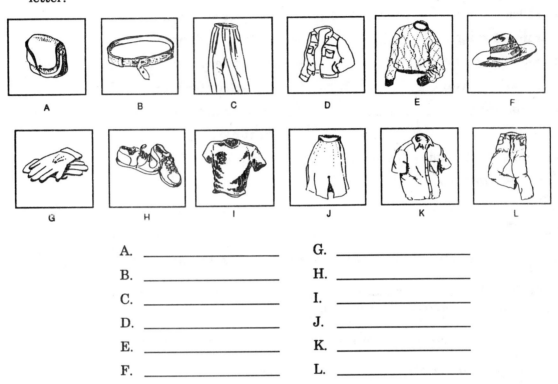

A. _____	G. _____
B. _____	H. _____
C. _____	I. _____
D. _____	J. _____
E. _____	K. _____
F. _____	L. _____

C. **Your teacher or peer partner will state the names of seven articles of clothing or accessories. After the second repetition, write the letter which corresponds to what you hear.**

1.___   2. ___   3. ___   4. ___   5. ___   6. ___   7. ___

D. **FIRST STUDY** Aim II, page 254, *Exercice oral 2.* Next complete the following statements with one or more appropriate articles of clothing or accessories.

1. **Quand il fait très froid mon oncle porte _____ et _____.**

2. **Quand il fait très chaud Anne porte _____ et _____.**

3. **Quand il pleut mon oncle porte _____ et _____.**

4. **Quand Joseph va à la plage il porte _____ et _____.**

5. **Quand Anne va à un mariage elle porte _____ et _____.**

6. **Quand ma tante va faire des courses elle porte _____.**

7. **Quand mon ami fait du sport il porte _____.**

8. **Quand Charles va à la remise des prix il porte _____ et _____.**

CORRECTIVE, UNIT X   NAME _____

II. Topic: *Quels vêtements est-ce que tu portes aujourd'hui?/ Et de quelle couleur...?*

A. FIRST STUDY Aim III, pages 257-258. Next read each of the following statements. If the statement is true, write *Vrai;* if the statement is false, write *Faux* and correct the bold part.

1. Le tableau est **noir**. _____
2. La craie est **rouge**. _____
3. Le papier est **blanc**. _____
4. L'arbre est **marron**. _____
5. La pomme est **grise**. _____

6. La laitue est **rose**. _____
7. La poire est **jaune**. _____
8. La carotte est **verte**. _____
9. Ma couleur favorite est **le bleu**. _____
10. Le drapeau américain est **rouge, blanc et orange**. _____

Quels vêtements est-ce que tu portes aujourd'hui? *(Write four articles of clothing you are wearing and the color of each article.)*

_____

_____

III. Topic: *Les couleurs* (Noun-Adjective Agreement)

A. FIRST STUDY *Exercice oral 3,* page 258 and read the examples given in the *Activités 1a. and 1b.* page 259.

B. Next write the **proper** form of the adjective in parenthesis in each sentence.

1. Ma tante porte un chemisier _____. (rose)
2. Mon père porte un chapeau _____. (noir)
3. Mes amis portent des chemises _____. (blanc)
4. Mes soeurs portent des vêtements _____. (rouge)
5. Mon frère porte un costume _____. (gris)
6. Jean et Joseph portent des cravates _____. (bleu)
7. Anne et Odile portent des manteaux _____. (vert)
8. Ma tante porte une jupe _____. (marron)

IV. Topic: *Une conversation au téléphone*

A. FIRST STUDY Aim I, *Exercice oral 2,* page 252 and *Vocabulaire,* pages 256, 268. Then write the **English meaning** of the following frequently used expressions.

1. Bonne idée ! _____
2. Merci. _____
3. Que tout se passe bien. _____
4. Quelle chance! _____
5. Remets-toi vite! _____
6. Comme je suis navré(e)! _____

7. De rien. _____
8. Je suis si contente! _____
9. Ne t'inquiéte pas! _____
10. Mon Dieu! _____
11. Je suis content(e)... _____
12. On va voir. _____

CORRECTIVE, UNIT X   NAME _____

IV. (continued)

13. Je ne peux pas... _____

14. J'ai besoin ... _____

15. Pourquoi n'allons-nous pas faire de courses?

     _____

16. Pourquoi n'allons-nous pas au cinéma?

     _____

17. Qu'est-ce qui se passe? _____

18. Tu as raison. _____

19. Faisons une promenade. _____

20. Je ne peux pas aller. _____

    B. Write an appropriate response from the choices given above to each of the following beginnings of telephone conversations.

1. C'est moi Hélène. Ma mère est malade. Elle est à l'hôpital.

    _____

2. C'est moi Jean. Le costume coûte cent quatre-vingts dollars.

    _____

3. C'est moi Raoul. J'ai deux mois de vacances.

    _____

4. C'est moi Barbara. Je ne peux pas aller à la partie. J'ai de la fievre.

    _____

5. C'est moi Marie. Je vais à la distribution des prix avec Pierre.

    _____

6. C'est moi Charles. Pourquoi n'allons nous pas au cinéma? Le film est bon.

    _____

7. C'est moi Anne. Je ne peux pas aller faire de courses. Je n'ai pas beaucoup d'argent.

    _____

CORRECTIVE, UNIT X   NAME _____

V. Topic: *La possession*

   A. FIRST STUDY Aim IV, pages 260-261.

   B. Answer the following questions according to the cues given. What word **do we use to** express possession in French? _____

1. A qui est cette maison? (Mme Guillou)

   _____

2. A qui est ce manteau? (mon frère)

   _____

3. A qui est cette voiture? (le professeur)

   _____

4. A qui est cette jaquette? (Claudine)

   _____

5. A qui sont ses chaussures? (ma soeur)

   _____

6. A qui sont ses stylos? (Robert)

   _____

7. A qui sont ses livres? (M. Plon)

   _____

VI. Topic: *Questions générales: "Aller faire des courses"*

   A. FIRST STUDY Aim V, page 262 and *Vocabulaire,* page 264.

   B. Then answer the following questions with a complete sentence in French.

1. Aimez-vous faire des courses? Pourquoi? _____

   _____

2. Avec qui allez-vous faire des courses? _____

   _____

3. Quand allez-vous faire des courses? _____

   _____

4. Comment allez-vous dans les magasins? _____

   _____

5. Où est-ce que vous achetez les vêtements? Pourquoi est-ce que vous achetez les vêtements là?

   _____

   _____

   _____

SITUATIONS ORALES, UNIT X   NAME _____

C. **Function:** Providing and Obtaining Information
   Role: I am your parent.
   Purpose: You are providing me with information as to the clothing you need to buy for school. You will begin the conversation.

D. **Function:** Expressing Feelings
   Role: I am your grandparent.
   Purpose: You want to tell me your feelings about a present I have just given you. I will begin the conversation.

E. **Function:** Persuasion
   Role: I am your best friend.
   Purpose: You wish to convince me to go shopping with you. You will begin the conversation.

NOTES

CORRECTIVE, UNIT XI   NAME _____

I. TOPIC: *Les endroits intéressants dans la capitale française*

A. FIRST STUDY Aim II, pages 280-289 and the*Vocabulaire,* pages 289-290.

B. Next fill in the **appropriate places** where John goes to do the following activities in Paris.

1. Pour acheter des timbres Jean va à la _____.

2. Pour prendre l'avion Jean va à _____Charles DeGaulle.

3. Pour voir un match to football Jean va au _____.

4. Pour voir un film Jean va au _____ Gaumont.

5. Pour voir un drame ou une comédie Jean va au _____ de la Comédie Française.

6. Pour voir de l'art Jean va au _____ du Louvre.

7. Pour voir une autre belle place Jean va _____.

8. Pour voir un très beau parc Jean va _____.

9. Pour lire des livres Jean va à la _____ Nationale.

10. Pour téléphoner en dehors de la ville de Paris Jean va à la _____.

11. Pour entendre la messe Jean va à la _____ Notre Dame de Paris.

12. Pour voir beaucoup d'animaux Jean va au _____ de Vincennes.

13. Pour voir un château impressionnant Jean va à _____.

C. Your teacher or peer partner will state a few places of interest in France's capital, Paris. After the second repetition, write the number from Part B (#1 - 14) which represents the purpose for which a person goes there.

Example: Le Zoo de Vincenne: *Answer #12* (Pour voir beaucoup d'animaux)

1.____   2.____   3.____   4. ____   5. ____   6. ____   7. ____

CORRECTIVE, UNIT XI   NAME _____

II. Topic: *La France et sa géographie*

A. FIRST READ Aim I, pages 275-277.

B. Next fill in the blank with the appropriate choice. Write the entire **word**, not the letter.

1. La France est _____.
   a. un continent   b. une région   c. une capitale   d. un pays

2. La France est dans le continent de _____.
   a. L'Asie   b. L'Afrique   c. L'Europe   d. L'Amérique

3. La capitale de la France est _____.
   a. Paris   b. Brest   c. Lyon   d. Marseille

4. Les pyrenées séparent la France de _____.
   a. L'Italie   b. La Suisse   c. L'Espagne   d. La Belgique

5. La Corse est dans _____.
   a. l'océan Atlantique   b. la Manche   c. la mer Mediterranée   d. la mer du Nord

6. Le Rhin est la frontière naturelle entre la France et _____.
   a. l'Espagne   b. La Suisse   c. l'Allemagne   d. L'Italie

7. Le fleuve qui passe à Paris est _____.
   a. la Loire   b. Le Rhône   c. la Garonne   d. La Seine

8. La langue officielle en France est _____ .
   a. le basque   b. le français   c. le breton   d. le provençal

9. Au sud de la France il y a le continent de _____.
   a. L'Europe   b. L'Asie   c. L'Afrique   d. L'Amérique

10. Le port industriel très important au sud de la France à l'embouchure de Rhône est _____.
   a. Brest   b. Cherbourg   c. Marseille   d. le Havre

CORRECTIVE, UNIT XI   NAME _____

III. Topic: *Voyager par le métro avec un plan*

A. FIRST READ Aim IIIB, *Lecture*, page 294.

B. Next STUDY the *Vocabulaire*, pages 295-296.

C. Then REVIEW Aim IIIC, page 297 while examining the map of the Métro on page 299.

D. Next write the instructions you would give to a stranger to get to the following places by Métro.

1. You are at the station *Montparnasse (ligne 4)* and s/he wants to go to the Zoo de Vincennes, station *Château de Vincennes*.

   _____

   _____

   _____

   _____

2. You are at the station *Charles de Gaulle (ligne 1)* and s/he wants to go to *Saint Michel,* station *Notre Dame*.

   _____

   _____

   _____

   _____

IV. *La pendule de 24 heures*

A. FIRST STUDY Aim IV, the *Note culturelle,* page 301.

B. Next write the following times of the 24 hour clock in time as used in the United States to indicate the departure or arrival times of the following trains or airplanes.

Examples:	8:15	huit heures et quart du matin
	16:40	cinq heures moins vingt de l'après-midi
	23:30	onze heures et demie du soir

1. 7:30 _____

2. 13:20 _____

3. 17:15 _____

4. 19:50 _____

5. 21:05 _____

6. 23:45 _____

132

CORRECTIVE, UNIT XI   NAME _____

V. Topic: *A quelle heure part le train? / A quelle heure arrive-t-il?*

A. First STUDY the *Exercice oral* page 302 while examining the railroad time schedule *Paris-Nord -- Tourcoing* on page 302.

B. Then answer the following questions while referring to the railroad time schedule *Paris-Nord -- Tourcoing* page 302. If the answer indicates a time between 12:59 p.m. and 12:00 midnight (12:00 a.m.), state the answer in two ways.

1a. A quelle heure part le train (#103) de Paris pour Tourcoing? _____
_____

1b. A quelle heure arrive-t-il à Tourcoing? _____
_____

2a. A quelle heure part le train (#2533) d'Amiens à Lille? _____
_____

2b. A quelle heure arrive-t-il à Lille? _____
_____

3a. A quelle heure part le train (#2033) de Paris à Amiens? _____
_____

3b. A quelle heure arrive-t-il à Amiens? _____
_____

4a. A quelle heure part le train (#522/3) de Longeau à Douai? _____
_____

4b. A quelle heure arrive-t-il a Douai? _____
_____

CORRECTIVE, UNIT XI   NAME _____

VI. Topic: Functions of language

A. Read Aim IIIB, *Lecture,* page 294 and study *Vocabulaire,* pages 295-296.

B. Read *Lecture,* page 305 and study *Vocabulaire,* page 307.

C. Write the following frequently used communicative phrases related to travel which appear in the *Lecture* in French.

1. Excuse me, Mr. / Miss / Mrs. _____

2. Where is the Métro station? _____

3. How can I get to the *Office de Tourisme?* _____

4. Thank you very much. You are very kind. _____

5. You're welcome. Thanks for your help. _____

6. How can I get to the railroad station? _____

7. I prefer to go by bus. _____

8. You have to (it is necessary to) take the Number 26 Bus. _____

   _____

9. Where is the nearest stop? _____

10. Go straight. It's on the corner. _____

11. How much does a bus ticket cost? _____

12. Can you tell me where the Information Counter is? _____

    _____

13. It's on the right (left). _____

14. At what time does the next train leave? _____

    _____

15. At what time does it arrive? _____

16. Here is a schedule for your next trip. _____

17. I want to buy one ticket, please. _____

CORRECTIVE, UNIT XI   NAME _____

VI. (continued)

D. Complete the following dialogue between the tourist and the stranger and the employee in Rome by writing the English phrases in French.

1. **Touriste:** _____, mademoiselle
   (Excuse me)

   _____ où est la gare de SNCF Montparnasse?
   (Can you tell me)

   Mademoiselle: Vous préférez aller en autobus ou par le métro?

2. **Touriste:** _____
   (I prefer to go by bus.)

   Mademoiselle: Il faut prendre le bus numéro 43.

3. **Touriste:** _____
   (Where is the nearest bus stop?)

   Mademoiselle: Allez tout droit. C'est au coin.

4. **Touriste:** _____
   (Thank you very much. You are very kind.)

   Mademoiselle: Je vous en prie.

   (Le touriste prend l'autobus et arrive à la station Montparnasse en une demi heure et cherche les renseignements.)

5. **Touriste:** Excusez-moi, Monsieur, _____
   (At what time does the next train leave for Brest?)

   Employé: A dix-sept heures quarante.

6. **Touriste:** _____
   (And at what time does it arrive?)

   Employé: A vingt-trois heures vingt-neuf.

7. **Touriste:** _____
   (How much does it cost?)

   Employé: 425.50 francs en première classe.

   (Le touriste va au guichet.)

8. **Touriste:** _____
   (One ticket for Brest, please.)

   Employé: Première ou deuxième classe?
9. **Touriste:** Première classe.
   Employé: Le voici.

10. **Touriste:** _____
    (Thank you.)

ENRICHMENT, UNIT XI   NAME _____

I.

During your first trip to France you and your friend decide to see as many places of interest as possible. You plan a five-day trip to the second city of France, Marseille. You go to the train station in Lyon (Lyon-Part-Dieu) to obtain a schedule of departures and arrivals. The SNCF employee at the information counter gives you a schedule called *Paris -- Nice-ville* and tells you that the train's time table is to be read from top to bottom following the cities from Paris down to Nice.

Paris --- Nice-ville

Numéro de train		5089	845	615	815	865	449/8	6173/2	6173/2	617	5051	5049	5289	819
Notes à consulter		1	2	3	4	5	6	7	8	9	10	11	12	13
			TGV	TGV	TGV	TGV				TGV				TGV
Paris-Gare-de-Lyon	D		10.41	11.00	11.40	11.45			12.00					12.55
Dijon-Ville	A		|	|	|	|			|					|
Macon-Ville	A		|	|	|	|			|					|
Lyon-Part-Dieu	A		12.45	13.02	|	|	13.50	13.50	14.02	14.06	14.11			|
Lyon-Perrache	A	12.31	|	13.10	|	|	|	|	14.10	|	|		|
Valence V	A	13.49	|		14.35	14.43	14.49	14.49		15.07	15.07		15.48
Orange	A	14.46	|		|	|	15.39	15.39		|	|		|
Avignon	A	15.06	|		15.30	15.34	15.58	15.58		16.10	16.10	16.25	16.45
Arles	A	15.26	|		|		|	|		16.31	16.31	17.20	|
Marseille-St-Charles	A	16.11	|		16.22		16.39	16.55	17.04	17.25	17.25		17.39
Cannes	A		17.10				18.39		19.17	19.36	19.36		
Juan-les-Pins	A		|				|		19.29	19.48	19.48		
Antibes	A		17.22				18.49		19.34	19.53	19.53		
Cagnes-sur-Mer	A		|				|		|	20.02	20.02		
Nice-Ville	A		17.38				19.05		19.53	20.16	20.16		

Les trains circulant tous les jours ont leurs horaires indiqués en gras
Tous les trains offrent des places assises en 1ʳᵉ et 2ᵉ classe, sauf indication contraire dans les notes.

ENRICHMENT, UNIT XI   NAME _____

I. (continued)

A.   Fill in the following outline to indicate the departure times from Lyon-Part-Dieu and the arrival times at Marseille for three trains. Give the hours of the 24-hour clock between 12:59 p.m. and midnight in two ways, using *"c'est à dire"* ("that is to say").

1. Le train (numéro) part de Lyon à _____,

    c'est à dire _____

    et arrive à Marseille à _____,

    c'est à dire _____.

2. Le train (numéro _____) part de Lyon à _____,

    c'est à dire, _____

    et arrive à Marseille à _____,

    c'est à dire _____.

B.   Now fill in the following outline to indicate the departure times from Marseille and the arrival times at Nice for three trains.

4. Le train (numéro _____) part de Marseille à _____,

    c'est à dire _____

    et il arrive à Nice à _____,

    c'est à dire _____.

5. Le train (numéro _____) part de Marseille à _____,

    c'est à dire _____

    et arrive à Nice à _____,

    c'est à dire _____.

6. Le train (numéro _____) part de Marseille à _____,

    c'est à dire _____

    et arrive à Nice à _____,

    c'est à dire _____.

ENRICHMENT, UNIT XI   NAME _____

II.

When you visit France you will probably fly into the country and then use the trains as a means of getting around. Read the following information about transportation and then answer the questions which follow.

1   Deux aéroports principaux désservent Paris: Charles de
2   Gaulle aéroport international à Roissy, et Orly.
3   Toutes les grandes lignes de la SNCF partent de Paris vers les
4   villes importantes de France et d'Europe. A Paris, il y a 6 gares
5   principales. Les gares de L'Est et du Nord comme l'indiquent
6   leurs noms désservent les villes du nord comme Lille, Calais,
7   Roubaix ainsi, que les Pays Bas, la Suède, le Danemark,
8   l'Angleterre et l'Allemagne.
9   Si l'on veut aller dans les villes et les régions de l'Ouest telles
10   que Brest, Quimper, Bordeaux, La Rochelle il faut prendre
11   le train à la gare Montparnasse.
12   Pour aller en Suisse, en Italie, à Lyon, à Marseille ainsi qu'à
13   Nice on part de la gare de Lyon. Pour les banlieux parisiennes et
14   la Normandie, c'est la gare Saint Lazare au centre de Paris, très
15   accessible à tous. Finalement, la gare d'Austerlitz vous
16   emmènera vers les châteaux de la Loire, Tours, Poitiers et les
17   porcelaines de Limoge.
18   La France continue d'être à l'avant garde du modernisme
19   dans les transports; le T.V.G. (train à grande vitesse) permet de
20   se rendre dans certaines grandes villes en un temps record. Par
21   exemple pour aller à Tours par le T.G.V., il faut 45 minutes. Par
22   le train normal il faut deux heures. Il y a deux T.G.V. en service.
23   Paris - Lyon ou le T.G.V. orange et Paris Rennes-Nante, T.G.V.
24   bleu/atlantique. La ligne Paris/Bordeaux est presque terminée. Il
25   ira jusqu'en Espagne.

Vocabulaire:

3. les grandes lignes *major lines*   SNFC (Société Nationale) *French national railroad*
vers *toward*
4. la gare *railroad station*
5. indiquer *to indicate*
6. désservir *to serve*
9. Si l'on veut aller *If one wants to go*
10. il faut prendre *one must take*
12. ainsi qu'à *as well as*
13. on part de *one leaves from*
14. très accessible *very accessible*
18. à l'avant garde *forward looking, modern*
19. T.G.V. (Train à grande vitesse) *very fast train*
20. temps record *record time*
24. il ira *it will go*

ENRICHMENT, UNIT XI   NAME _____

II. (cont.)

Questions sur la lecture:

1. Les deux aéroports principaux de Paris s'appellent _____

   et _____.

2. Comment s'appellent les chemins de fer français? _____

   _____

3. Combien est-ce qu'il y a de gares à Paris? _____

4. Comment s'appellent-elles?

   _____   _____

   _____   _____

   _____   _____

5. Le train à grande vitesse s'appelle _____

6. Donnez le nom des deux T.G.V. _____

   _____

Let's take a trip from Paris

1. John wants to go to Amsterdam. From which train station should he depart?

   _____

2. Paul decides to go to London for the Christmas holiday. From which station should he depart?

   _____

3. From which station would you leave for a skiing vacation in Switzerland?

   _____

4. If your French penpal wants to come to the United States to visit you, which major Paris airport would most likely be used? _____

SITUATIONS ORALES, UNIT XI   NAME _____

A. **Function:** Socializing
   Role: I am seated next to you on a plane to Paris.
   Purpose: We are talking about our trip to France and what we will be doing there. I will begin the conversation.

1. **Passager:** Combien de temps allez-vous passer à Paris?

   Vous: _____

2. **Passager:** Où est votre hôtel?

   Vous: _____

3. **Passager:** Quels sont les endroits intéressants à Paris?

   Vous: _____

4. **Passager:** Comment voyagez-vous dans Paris?

   Vous: _____

5. **Passager:** Où allez-vous faire des achats à Paris?

   Vous: _____

6. **Passager:** Où préférez-vous manger?

   Vous.: _____

B. **Function:** Providing and Obtaining Information
   Roles: I am an employee at the ticket window of the SNCF in Paris.
   Purpose: You want to find out about the schedule and cost for a trip to Lyon for you and a friend. You will begin the conversation.

1. **Vous:** _____?

   L'employé: Le prochain train pour Lyon part à onze heures.

2. **Vous:** _____?

   L'employé: Le train arrive à Lyon à quatorze heures vingt.

3. **Vous:** _____?

   L'employé: Un billet de première classe coûte 2685 francs.

4. **Vous:** _____?

   L'employé: En deuxième classe c'est 2100 francs.

5. **Vous:** _____.

   L'employé: Voici l'argent.

SITUATIONS ORALES, UNIT XI   NAME _____

C. **Function:** Expressing Personal Feelings
   Role: I am your travel agent.
   Purpose: Express your ideas about an ideal vacation. You will begin the conversation by telling me where you want to travel.

D. **Function:** Providing and Obtaining Information
   Roles: I am a Customs Inspector.
   Purpose: You have just arrived in my country and I wish to find out some information about you and the purpose of your trip. I will begin the conversation.

E. **Function:** Persuasion
   Roles: We are friends who are traveling together in Paris.
   Purpose: We have only one day left in Paris before our flight home. Convince me to go to a place that you would like to visit.

CORRECTIVE, UNIT XII   NAME _____

I. Topic: *Les magasins en France*

A. FIRST STUDY Aim I, pages 311-316 Read and review *Notes culturelles* page 315-316.

B. Next fill in the blank with the product sold in each of the following places. Choices are given.

1. Dans la boucherie _____.
2. Dans la poissonnerie on vend _____.
3. Dans le kiosque on vend _____ et _____.
4. Dans la boulangerie on vend _____.
5. Dans la pâtisserie on vend _____.
6. Dans la pharmacie on vend _____.
7. Dans le magasin de chaussures on vend _____.
8. Dans l'épicerie on vend _____.
9. Dans la librairie on vend _____.
10. Dans la charcuterie on vend _____.
11. Dans le magasin de confection on vend _____.
12. Dans la parfumerie on vend _____.

Choices:
les livres	la nourriture	les parfums
le poisson	les vêtements	les médicaments
les chaussures	les gâteaux	le pain
la viande	les fruits	les magazines et journaux

CORRECTIVE, UNIT XII   NAME _____

II. Topic: *La culture*

A. Read carefully *Notes culturelles,* pages 315 and 316.

B. Next fill in the blank with an appropriate word or expression.

1. In the épicerie one can buy (3 things) _____.

2. To buy medicines you would have to go to _____.

3. To buy cakes you would have to go to _____.

4. Where can you buy shellfish? _____.

5. What is the equivalent of *la charcuterie*? _____.

6. Where would you buy a postcard? _____.

7. Shoe sizes in France follow the measurement system called _____.

8. Most stores in France (except the large department stores) are closed between the hours of

    _____.

9. What is le "Marché?" _____.

CORRECTIVE, UNIT XII   NAME _____

III. Topic: *Les métiers dans la communauté*

A. FIRST STUDY Aim IIIA, pages 320-324. Next write the job or work the person does in the community under each picture.

 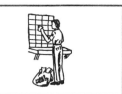 

_____ _____ _____ _____

B. For each of the following job descriptions, write the person who does the work described in the blank provided.

1. _____ vend le pain dans la boulangerie.

2. _____ examine les malades dans le bureau de consultations.

3. _____ éteind les feux dans les bâtiments.

4. _____ ramasse les ordures dans la rue.

5. _____ s'occupe des enfants et nettoie la maison.

6. _____ aide les gens dans la rue.

7. _____ enseigne aux enfants à l'école.

8. _____ vend des vêtements dans le magasin de vêtements.

9. _____ prépare des programmes pour la compagnie.

10. _____ distribue les lettres dans les maisons.

11. _____ vend la viande dans la boucherie.

12. _____ défend les clients au tribunal.

13. _____ tape à la machine dans un bureau.

14. _____ conduit un autobus dans la ville.

C. Topic: *Mon future métier* FIRST STUDY Aim IIIB, pages 324-327. Next answer the questions.

Que veux-tu faire? Pourquoi? _____

_____

_____

CORRECTIVE, UNIT XII   NAME _____

IV. Topic: *Mon quartier et ma ville*

A. FIRST STUDY Aim II, pages 317-319. Read page 317 carefully and study the *Vocabulaire*, page 319.

B. Next answer the following questions with a complete sentence in French.

1. Comment est la ville où tu vis? _____

   _____

2. Combien est-ce qu'il y a d'habitants? _____

   _____

3. Comment est le quartier où tu vis? _____

   _____

   _____

4. Est-ce que tu vis près ou loin des magasins? _____

   _____

5. Quels sont les magasins principaux de ton quartier? _____

   _____

   _____

6. Dans quels magasins est-ce que tu vas souvent? _____

   _____

7. Avec qui est-ce que tu vas dans les magasins? _____

   _____

8. Est-ce qu'il y a quelque chose d'historique dans ta ville? Qu'est-ce que c'est?_____

   _____

   _____

9. Quels sont les endroits intéressants et de récréation dans ta ville? _____

   _____

   _____

ENRICHMENT, UNIT XII   NAME _____

I. Puzle

Can you find the nine jobs or professions hidden in this word search? As you find one, circle it, and write each one in the blanks provided.

```
R  S  A  D  F  A  C  T  E  U  R
S  E  B  C  I  F  G  K  B  M  V
T  C  V  E  N  H  R  L  O  N  E
U  R  E  J  F  I  Q  P  U  O  T
D  E  N  T  I  S  T  E  E  S  E
V  T  D  E  R  N  U  S  U  R  R
W  A  E  A  M  A  B  D  R  M  I
O  I  U  V  I  L  Z  V  E  N  N
P  R  R  O  E  H  M  S  O  Q  A
Q  E  W  C  R  Z  R  U  V  T  I
M  E  C  A  N  I  C  I  E  N  R
F  A  M  T  R  L  O  B  A  D  E
```

1. _____
2. _____
3. _____
4. _____
5. _____
6. _____
7. _____
8. _____
9. _____

II. Qui suis-je?

The following people are describing their jobs and careers. Fill in each blank with the appropriate name of each person's job.

1. Je travaille dans un bureau. Les clients viennent me voir quand ils ont des problèmes avec les dents. Je suis _____.

2. Je travaille dans un bureau pour une grande compagnie. Je prépare des programmes. Je suis _____.

3. Je travaille dans un garage. Je répare les voitures. Je suis _____.

4. Je travaille dans un bureau. Je tape à la machine et je réponds au téléphone. Je suis _____.

5. Je travaille dans un bureau et aussi au tribunal. Je défends mes clients. Je suis _____.

6. Je travaille dans la rue. Je ramasse les ordures des immeubles. Je suis _____.

7. Je travaille dans un hôpital pour animaux. Je m'occupe des animaux malades. Je suis _____.

8. Je travaille dans un hôpital. J'aide et je m'occupe des malades. Je suis _____.

9. Je travaille à la maison. Je m'occupe de mes enfants. Je fais la cuisine et je nettoie la maison. Je suis _____.

10. Je conduis un autobus dans les rues de la ville. Je suis _____.

Vocabulaire:
3. réparer   *to fix*
4. taper à la machine   *to typewrite*   5. le tribunal   *court*   6. ramasser   *to pick up*
10. conduire   *to drive*

ENRICHMENT, UNIT XII

NAME _____

III. Pour gagner ma vie je...

Write a one or two sentence description in French of what the following people do *to earn a living*. Be sure to state where each person works.

1. Je suis professeur. Je _____

    _____

2. Je suis docteur. Je _____

    _____

3. Je suis vendeuse de vêtements. Je _____

    _____

4. Je suis facteur. Je _____

    _____

5. Je suis pompier. Je _____

    _____

IV. Il y a tant de carrières

There are so many careers to choose from. Make a list of some careers and jobs that have the following characteristics.

1. Les carrières dans lesquelles on travaille avec les mains:

    _____, _____, et _____

2. Les carrières dans lesquelles on travaille avec les machines:

    _____, _____, et _____

3. Les carrières dans lesquelles on travaille avec des enfants ou des adolescents:

    _____, _____, et _____

4. Les carrières dans lesquelles on travaille avec des malades:

    _____, _____, et _____

5. Les carrières dans lesquelles il est important de parler une autre langue:

    _____, _____, et _____

Vocabulaire:

pompier   *fireman*

une carrière   *a job*

ENRICHMENT, UNIT XII   NAME _____

V. *Comment veux-tu gagner ta vie?* (How do you want to earn a living?)

Answer the following questions related to your future work in complete sentences in French.

1. **Que veux-tu faire? Pourquoi?** _____

   _____

2. **Où est-ce que tu veux travailler?** _____

   _____

3. **Est-ce que tu veux travailler seul(e) ou avec d'autres personnes?** _____

   _____

4. **Est-ce que tu préfères travailler avec la tête ou avec les mains?** _____

   _____

5. **Est-ce que tu aimes aider les gens dans leur travail?** _____

   _____

6. **Est-ce que tu voudrais travailler pour une grande compagnie ou à ton compte?** _____

   _____

7. **Est-ce que c'est important pour toi** *(for you)* **de gagner beaucoup d'argent dans ton travail?**

   _____

   _____

Vocabulaire:

6: à ton compte   *on your own*
7: pour moi   *for me*
   pour toi   *for you*
   gagner beaucoup d'argent   *to earn a lot of money*

ENRICHMENT, UNIT XII   **NAME** _____

VI.

Read the following narration told by Christian Gac. The first time read to understand the general meaning. The second time read to find the answers to the questions which follow.

1   Je m'apelle Christian Gac. Je suis de Belgique. J'ai vingt-quatre ans. J'habite dans le Bronx
2   dans la ville de New York avec mes parents et deux soeurs. Cela fait dix ans que j'habite dans
3   cette ville.
4   J'habite au onzième étage d'un immeuble qui a vingt étages. Mon appartement est grand et
5   confortable. Il y a trois chambres à coucher, une salle de séjour, deux salles de bain, une salle à
6   manger et une cuisine. J'aime mon quartier parce-qu'il est près d'un joli parc. Au printemps il y a
7   des fleurs dans les jardins et beaucoup d'écureuils dans le parc. Le dimanche, en été, mes parents
8   emmènent des chaises au parc pour s'asseoir au soleil. Quelquefois quand il fait très chaud, il
9   s'asseyent sous les arbres. En automne j'aime voir les feuilles qui changent de couleurs. En hiver,
10   quand il neige beaucoup, les enfants du quartier vont au parc jouer avec la neige.
11   Il y a peu de magasins dans le quartier. Il y a un supermarché, une banque, une pizzéria, une
12   pharmacie, un coiffeur et une teinturerie. Quand ma mère veut acheter de la nourriture, mon père
13   l'emmène en voiture dans un grand supermarché près d'ici. Quand elle veut acheter des
14   vêtements elle va en ville parce qu'il y a beaucoup de magasins et elle y trouve tout ce qu'elle
15   veut.
16   Je travaille dans un bureau pour une grande compagnie à Manhattan. Je suis programmateur
17   pour ordinateurs. J'aime beaucoup aller en ville parce-qu'il y a beaucoup de restaurants, théâtres,
18   cinémas, discothèques et musées. A la fin de la semaine je vais danser dans les discothèques. Dans
19   beaucoup d'endroits à New York on joue de la musique moderne. En été quand il fait beau, mes
20   amis et moi nous allons au Parc Central à Manhattan pour jouer au baseball. Pendant la saison
21   de baseball nous allons aussi au stade de baseball pour voir jouer les équipes de baseball de New
22   York.
23   Quand mes cousins de Belgique viennent me rendre visite, je les emmène voir les merveilles de
24   New York: La Statue de la Liberté, Les Nations-Unies, "L'Empire State," Le Centre Rockefeller,
25   la Cathédrale Saint Patrick, le Centre Lincoln, Les Tours Jumelles, et le Zoo du Bronx. Quand ma
26   tante favorite qui est maîtresse en Belgique vient nous voir nous allons toujours au Musée d'Art
27   Metropolitain et au Musée d'Art Moderne. J'aime ma ville adoptive "la Grosse Pomme."

Vocabulaire:
7. un écureuil   *squirrel*
8. emmener   *to carry, to take something, someone*
    s'asseoir   *to sit down* (irregular conjugation): je m'assieds, tu t'assieds, il/elle s'assied, nous nous
    asseyons, vous vous asseyez, ils/elles s'asseyent
9. les feuilles qui changent de couleurs   *the change of color of the leaves*
10. il neige   *it snows:* neiger   *to snow*
12. le coiffeur   *hairdresser*   une teinturerie   *drycleaner's shop*
13. il l'emmène   *he takes her*
14. en ville   *downtown, in the center*   elle y trouve   *there she finds*
    tout ce qu'elle veut   *all that she wants*
16. programmateur   *computer programmer*
19. l'endroit   *the place*
20. la saison de   *the season of*
23. je les emmène   I *take them:* j'emmène, tu emmènes, il/elle emmène, nous emmenons, vous
    emmenez, ils/elles emmènent
25. les Tours Jumelles   *The Twin Towers (World Trade Center)*
26. le maître (la maîtresse)   *elementary school teacher*

ENRICHMENT, UNIT XII   NAME _____

VI. *Questions à répondre*

Answer the following questions with a complete sentence in French.

1. D'où est Christian Gac? _____
2. Avec qui est-ce qu'il vit? _____
_____
3. Combien d'étages y-a-t-il dans l'immeuble où il vit? _____
_____
4. A quel étage habite Christian? _____
5. Pourquoi est-ce que Christian aime son quartier? _____
_____
6. Quand est-ce que ses parent vont s'asseoir du soleil? _____
_____
7. Que font les enfants du quartier en hiver? _____
_____
8. Quels sont les magasins de son quartier? _____
_____
9. Qui emmène sa mère acheter la nourriture? _____
_____
10. Quand est-ce que sa mère va en ville? _____
_____
11. Où est-ce que Christian travaille? _____
_____
12. Pourquoi est-ce que Christian aime aller en ville? _____
_____
13. Quand va-t-il danser? _____
14. Que font Christian et ses amis quand il fait beau? _____
_____
15. Où est-ce que Christian emmène ses cousins? _____
_____
16. Qui est-ce que Christian emmène aux musées? _____
_____
17. Est-ce que Christian aime la ville de New York? _____
_____

ENRICHMENT, UNIT XII   NAME _____

VII.

Read the following dialogue in which Odile goes to the market to buy the food necessary to cook an American meal for her French family. Then answer the questions which follow in a complete sentence in French.

Lecture: *Première partie*

Un jour Odile décide de préparer un repas typiquement américain pour la famille française avec qui elle vit.

1 **Odile:** Demain dimanche j'aimerais préparer un repas pour la famille.
2 **Mme Durand:** Et qu'est-ce que tu veux préparer?
3 **Odile:** Je veux préparer un repas américain: hamburgers, frites, salade et
4   pour le dessert, une tarte aux pommes.
5 **Mme Durand:** Formidable! Est-ce que je peux t'aider?
6 **Odile:** A quelle heure ouvre la boucherie?
7 **Mme Durand:** Elle ouvre à neuf heures.
8 **Odile:** Et aujourd'hui samedi, à quelle heure est-ce qu'elle ferme?
9 **Mme Durand:** Elle ferme à midi et demie et elle n'ouvre pas l'après-midi.
10 **Odile:** Et où achetez-vous les légumes et les fruits?
11 **Mme Durand:** Le meilleur endroit c'est le marché ici dans le quartier où on achète tout très
12   frais.
13 **Odile:** Combien de viande hâchée est-ce que je dois acheter?
14 **Mme Durand:** Tu dois en acheter un kilo et demi.
15 **Odile:** Est-ce que je dois acheter de l'huile?
16 **Mme Durand:** Non, j'en ai assez.
17 **Odile:** Et combien de kilos de pommes de terre est-ce que je dois acheter?
18 **Mme Durand:** Deux kilos.
19 **Odile:** Il est neuf heures et quart. D'abord je vais au marché parce-que c'est déjà ouvert.
20   A bientôt, Mme Durand.
21 **Mme Durand:** Au revoir.

Vocabulaire:

5. Formidable   *great, wonderful*
6. à quelle heure ouvre?   *at what time does ... open?*
10. les légumes   *vegetables*
11. le meilleur endroit   *the best place*
12. frais   *fresh*
13. combien   *how much*   la viande hâchée   *chopped meat*
    je dois   *I must, should, ought to*

14. un kilo   *a kilogram (metric measurement equal to 2.2 pounds)*

19. est ouvert   *is open*   déjà   *already*

ENRICHMENT, UNIT XII   NAME _____

VII. (continued)

Questions à répondre: répondez aux questions par une phrase complete en Français.

1. Avec qui est-ce qu'Odile vit? _____

2. Qu'est-ce qu'Odile décide de préparer? _____
    _____

3. Où est-ce que Mme Durand achète la viande? _____

4. A quelle heure ouvre la boucherie? _____

5. A quelle heure est-ce que la boucherie ferme le samedi? _____
    _____

6. Où est-ce que Mme Durand achète les fruits et les légumes? _____
    _____

7. Combien de viande hachée est-ce qu'Odile doit acheter? _____
    _____

8. Est-ce qu'Odile doit acheter de l'huile? Pourquoi? _____
    _____

9. Combien de kilos de pommes de terre est-ce qu'Odile doit acheter? _____
    _____

10. Pourquoi est-ce qu'Odile va au marché en premier? _____
    _____

Lecture: deuxième partie

Odile entre dans le marché et regarde les différents stands. Dans l'un d'eux elle voit des pommes très jolies et pas chères.

1 **Odile:** Bonjour, Monsieur.
2 **Vendeur:** Bonjour, Mademoiselle. Que désirez-vous?
3 **Odile:** Deux kilos de pommes.
4 **Vendeur:** Vous désirez autre chose?
5 **Odile:** Je veux aussi deux kilos de pommes de terre, un kilo de tomates mûres,
6   une laitue et une livre d'oignons.
7 **Vendeur:** Autre chose?
8 **Odile:** C'est tout, merci. Ça fait combien?
9 **Vendeur:** 78.50 francs.
10 **Odile:** Voici un billet de 100 francs.
11 **Vendeur:** Et voilà votre monnaie. Merci.
12 **Odile:** Où est-ce que je peux acheter du pain pour hamburgers?
13 **Vendeur:** Le stand qui vend ce pain est fermé aujourd'hui. Vous pouvez aller au supermarché
14   à côté des Galeries Lafayette.
15 **Odile:** Merci beaucoup, Monsieur.
16 **Vendeur:** A votre service.

ENRICHMENT, UNIT XII   NAME _____

VII. (continued)

Odile va au supermarché à côté des Galeries Lafayette pour acheter le pain et 400 grammes de fromage. Puis elle rentre à la maison très contente parce qu'elle a tout ce qui est nécéssaire pour le repas de dimanche.

Vocabulaire:

         le stand   *stand where something is sold*
15. mûre   *ripe*
8. ça fait combien?   *How much is it?*
10. Voici un billet de   *Here is a ... bill.*
11. la monnaie   *change*
13. est fermé   *is closed*
         un gramme   *a gram - when shopping for small quantities, French people usually order by the 100 grams, about 3 1/2 ounces*
         rentrer   *to return:* elle rentre   *returns*
         tout ce qui est nécéssaire   *all which is necessary*
         Note: un livre   *a book*
                une livre   *a pound (of anything)*

Questions à répondre: Répondez aux questions par une phrase complète en français.

1. Que voit Odile à un des stands du marché? _____

_____

2. Combien de kilos de pommes est-ce qu'Odile achète? _____

_____

3. Qu'est-ce qu'Odile achète d'autre? _____

4. Combien coûte le tout? _____

5. Combien d'argent est-ce qu'Odile donne au vendeur? _____

_____

6. Combien d'argent est-ce que le vendeur rend à Odile? _____

_____

7. Pourquoi est-ce qu'Odile ne peut pas acheter le pain pour les hamburgers au marché? _____

_____

8. Quand est-ce qu'Odile va préparer le repas pour la famille? _____

_____

Vocabulaire:

4. Combien coûte le tout?   *How much for all this?*

6. devoir de l'argent   *to owe money*

    rendre de l'argent   *to return money or to return the change*

ENRICHMENT, UNIT XII   NAME _____

VII. (continued)

Questions à répondre: Répondez aux questions par une phrase complète en français.

1. Est-ce que vous achetez la nourriture pour votre famille quelquefois? _____
   _____

2. Où est-ce que vous achetez la nourriture? _____
   _____

3. A quelle heure ouvre le supermarché ou le marché dans votre quartier? _____
   _____

4. A quelle heure ferme-t-il? _____

5. Est-ce que le supermarché est ouvert le dimanche? _____
   _____

6. Est-ce que la pizzéria est ouverte le dimanche? _____
   _____

7. Est-ce que la poste est fermée le samedi et le dimanche? _____
   _____

8. Quels magasins sont fermés le dimanche? _____
   _____

9. Quels magasins sont ouverts le dimanche? _____
   _____

10. Quels sont les horaires des magasins de votre quartier pendant la semaine?
    _____
    _____

Vocabulaire:

l'horaire   *the hours for opening and closing in various establishments*

VIII. *Annonces d'emploi* (Advertisements for jobs)

Read the following classified ads for jobs from a newspaper in Paris and then answer the following questions in English.

Université US cherche
pour son centre de Paris
prof. avec Ph. D., nat. US
pour développement réseau
EEC et rel. pub. Part time
job. Ecrire à PROMO J,
15, rue de Paris, 92100
Boulogne avec réf. LM28
sur env., qui transmettra.

1a. Who can apply for this job? _____

1b. What language would be required? _____

1c. What kind of job is it? _____

Centre de promotion
international
pour la diffusion
d'un produit très performant
importé des USA
RECHERCHE
sur la FRANCE (toutes régions)
et à l'ÉTRANGER

PERSONNES (H/F)

dynamiques et entreprenantes.
Capables de recruter et diriger
des groupes de distributeurs
indépendants.
A temps partiel ou complet.
FORMATION COMPLÈTE
ASSURÉE
Prière d'adr. CV + courrier au
MONDE PUBLICITÉ
sous n° 8585
15/17, rue du Col.-Pierre-Avia
75902 Paris cedex 15

2a. From where is the product to be marketed? _____

2b. What qualities should the person applying have? _____

_____

2c. Is it a full or part time job? _____

2d. Is training being offered? _____

ÉDITEUR

recherche

2 COLLABORATRICES

libres rapidement
pour assurer démarches
annonceurs dans
revue professionnelle
bonne culture générale
indispensable

Se présenter : mercredi,
jeudi, vendredi : 15 h à 18 h.
« Formes et structures »
9, rue de Trévise,
75009 Paris.

3a. Who is looking for 2 collaborators? _____

3b. What is indispensible? _____

3c. What time and days are the interviews? _____

VIII. *Annonces d'emploi* (Advertisements for jobs, cont'd)

ENCYCLOPAEDIA UNIVERSALIS
Recherche
COLLABORATEURS
H ou F
Bon niveau de culture
générale pour poste à
caractère commercial
(pas de porte à porte)
– Formation assurée
– Rémunération très moti-
vante comportant un mini-
mum garanti
– Évolution de carrière rapide
pour candidat de valeur.
Tél. : 47-54-99-18.

4a. What are they selling? _____

4b. Are they selling door-to-door? _____

4c. Are they training the applicants? _____

4d. How is the pay? _____

4e. Can the candidate advance rapidly in the position? _____

_____

AGENCE DE PUBLICITÉ
par l'objet
recherche

VRP EXCLUSIFS

Sur Normandie et
Ile-de-France.
Env. lettre, CV, prét. à :
IDEACTION
BP 513
27135 Verneuil-sur-Avre.

5a. What kind of agency is this? _____

5b. Is this position for Paris or another region? _____

_____

5c. Where does the candidate send the letter or CV (curriculum vitae)?

_____

IMPORTANTE SOCIÉTÉ
DE SERVICES rech.

JURISTE
DROIT DES AFFAIRES
Haut Niveau
Libre rapidement.
Pouvant se déplacer.
Env. lettre man. CV photo
et prét. s/réf. 4434.
AFFLUENTS, 43, r. Chemin-Vert
Paris 11ᵉ qui trans.

6a. What is this postition for? _____

6b. What is necessary for this position? _____

6c. What references must be sent? _____

SITUATIONS ORALES, UNIT XII   NAME _____

A. **Function:** Expressing feelings
   Role: I am your parent.
   Purpose: Express your ideas about an ideal job. I will begin the conversation.

1. **Mère/Père:** Quel travail aimerais-tu faire?

   Toi: _____

2. **Mère/Père:** Où aimerais-tu travailler?

   Toi: _____

3. **Mère/Père:** Qu'est-ce que tu fais dans ce travail?

   Toi: _____

4. **Mère/Père:** Pourquoi est-ce que tu aimes faire ce travail?

   Toi: _____

5. **Mère/Père:** A quelle université vas-tu aller?

   Toi: _____

B. **Function:** Providing and Obtaining Information
   Roles: We are friends from the old neighborhood.
   Purpose: You have moved and I want to find out about your new city and neighborhood.
   I will begin the conversation.

1. **Moi:** Comment est la ville de...?

   Toi: _____

2. **Moi:** Combien d'habitants est-ce qu'il y a dans la ville?

   Toi: _____

3. **Moi:** Comment est le quartier où tu vis?

   Toi: _____

4. **Moi:** Quels sont les différents magasins de ton quartier?

   Toi: _____

5. **Moi:** Avec qui est-ce que tu vas dans les magasins (à la pizzéria)?

   Toi: _____

6. **Moi:** Quels endroits intéressants et de rècréations y-a-t-il dans ta ville?

   Toi: _____

C. **Function:** Providing and Obtaining Information
   Role: I work in the department of personnel and interview prospective job candidates.
   Purpose: You are seeking a job in my company. I will begin the conversation.

D. **Function:** Persuasion
   Role: I am your best friend.
   Purpose: You have just moved to a city in another state. You are so happy with your new
   neighborhood that you try to convince me to move there too.
   You will begin the conversation.

NOTES

NOTES

NOTES

NOTES